Homosexuality
and Christian
Community

Homosexuality
and Christian
Community

Edited by
Choon-Leong Seow

 Westminster John Knox Press
Louisville, Kentucky

Book design by Jennifer K. Cox
Cover design by Kevin Darst

First edition

Published by Westminster John Knox Press
Louisville, Kentucky

This book is printed on acid-free paper that meets the American National Standards Institute Z39.48 standard. ∞

PRINTED IN THE UNITED STATES OF AMERICA

96 97 98 99 00 01 02 03 04 05 — 10 9 8 7 6 5 4 3 2

Library of Congress Cataloging-in-Publication Data

Homosexuality and Christian community / Choon-Leong Seow, editor. — 1st ed.
    p.   cm.
Includes bibliographical references.
ISBN 0-664-25664-3 (alk. paper)
    1. Homosexuality—Religious aspects—Christianity.
2. Homosexuality—Biblical teaching.   I. Seow, C. L. (Choon-Leong)
BR115.H6H63   1996
261.8′35766—dc20   95-46242

Contents

Introduction

The biblical community of faith is a lively and dynamic one. It is neither static nor monolithic. Throughout history, people of this community have endeavored to articulate their convictions "in many and various ways"—to use the words of the writer of the epistle to the Hebrews. When we read the scriptures, therefore, we overhear spirited conversations regarding critical theological and ethical matters.

Within the Bible we discern certain voices that stress the transcendence of God, a God who is Wholly Other, while others emphasize the immanence of God, a God who is with us and deigns to be in relationship with humanity. Amid persistent faith in divine presence, we also hear within the same community the cries of those who experience God's absence. Together with the hymns of praise and thanksgiving, there are also heartfelt laments.

Some voices in the scriptures speak of the covenant in terms of an eternally valid promise, unilaterally given by God, while others present the covenant as a bilateral and conditional treaty between God and a particular people. The former model of the covenant calls attention to God's sheer grace—the fact that God will save, protect, and bless people even while they are unaware. The latter emphasizes human freedom to respond in obedience to God's imperatives or to reject them and face the consequences.

In most of the Bible we find a "theology from above" that begins with revelation and the will of God. We also find, however, a focus in the wisdom literature on humanity and the world at large, with due consideration for human knowledge gained through observation of nature and experience. Inasmuch as its emphasis is on the potentialities and limitations of human discovery, wisdom is a veritable "theology from below," one that stands in stark contrast to the dominant and more well-known "theology from above." The teachers in this tradition were concerned mostly with "this-worldly" matters, things that concern people in their present experiences, in their everyday lives. At the same time, one also finds in the Bible a tradition that points to "otherworldly" matters, a tradition—typified by the books of Daniel and Revelation—that is concerned with God's secrets and mysteries that are decided in the heavenly realm and determined for a time yet to come. In the New Testament we find Paul's theology of justification by grace alone through faith, but we also find the perspective of James that "faith without works is dead." These are some of the many conversations that we overhear in the scriptures.

Indeed, we affirm that God has spoken to our spiritual forebears "in many and various ways." That variety is perhaps necessitated by the limitations of our humanity. We are finite, while God is infinite; the finite cannot contain the infinite. No single perspective is adequate to convey the realities of human experiences of God, and any point of view, if overemphasized and absolutized, distorts the reality. So we listen to the living Word of God that has come through these many conversations, and we recognize, too, that inasmuch as human beings are finite, every human attempt to articulate truth about God, every formulation of faith, is necessarily provisional and contingent, subject to confirmation or challenge. This is also evident in the conversations within the scriptures, for the biblical theologians constantly refined and reformulated their convictions as they encountered ever anew the reality of God. The conversations in the Bible, therefore, have continued from generation to generation, as the faithful in each period of history sought to convey their experiences of God in light of their own times and places.

Likewise, we in the community of faith today are not a passive audience to the biblical conversations of long ago. We do not merely report or regurgitate what we overhear in the scriptures. As heirs of the traditions and members of the faith community, we must participate in the ongoing dialogue in order to discern the Word of the living God for our time.

The conversations have continued, as they should, beyond the biblical world, throughout the history of the church, and even to our own generation. Along with other mainline denominations, the Presbyterian Church (U.S.A.) has been struggling with a number of controversial issues in recent years, particularly the question of the ordination of self-avowed, practicing gays and lesbians to the ministry, the blessing of homosexual unions, liturgical and theological language about God, and the role of the church in a pluralistic world. Passions run high as we engage one another in the debates, and each side claims to be more "faithful" to the calling of the church. Here, too, we are all—no matter where we stand on any issue—heirs of the biblical traditions.

Two general perspectives emerge in these dialogues. On the one hand, there are those of us who believe that nothing less than the survival of the faith is at stake. In this scriptural tradition, the failure to maintain the standards of conduct that the community of faith has long recognized to be normative would compromise the church's unique identity as a covenant people. And it is this covenant faithfulness that distinguishes us from others. When the community of faith surrenders its allegiance to the God of the covenant by worshiping idols, either literally or figuratively, it ceases to be in right relationship with God. The covenant is broken. Moreover, the community is called to believe a God who has created the world in a manner consistent with divine will; human beings, in the image of God, are called to be stewards in the created order. Throughout its history the people of God have been tempted to dilute the divine commandments and assimilate into popular culture or to disregard their own creatureliness. But the faithful must resist such temptations. The church is, after all, called to be different; it is a community that has been called out to be in the world but not of the world. We are called to obey a God who commands the covenant community to rid itself of every unsavory influence that might lead it to apostasy and the dishonor of God. We worship a God whose name is Jealous, a God who brooks no compromise.

On the other hand, there are those of us who are equally convinced that the authenticity of the church is in question if it is unchanging and exclusivistic. Again, nothing less than the survival of the faith is at stake for us. In this scriptural tradition, the church is unfaithful if it turns its back on those who are marginalized in various ways by society or if the church itself excludes people on the basis of their race, gender, or sexual orientation from full participation in its life and leadership. We proclaim the good news that salvation has come to us not only through the familiar ancestors like Abraham, Isaac, and Jacob, but also through people who are perceived by the community as "unacceptable" outsiders: Tamar the Canaanite, who had sex with her father-in-law; Rahab, the Canaanite prostitute; Ruth, the foreign wife; Uriah's wife, who committed adultery with David; and a young unwed mother named Mary. This is, indeed, the beginning of the gospel, the good news that God comes to us in ways that totally surprise and often scandalize us; through an infant born in a stable, through a man rejected by his people and crucified like a common thief, through those who are marginalized. The church is called to be a community that manifests the inclusive grace and love of God. In the language of the Bible, we worship a God whose name is Compassionate, a God who is sovereign and free to extend grace to any and all.

The Christian community at Princeton Theological Seminary also is engaging in such conversations. In the spring of 1993, a number of people in this community issued a document titled "A Princeton Declaration: Upholding the PC(USA) in the Decision Not to Ordain Individuals Engaged in Homosexual Practice." The signers of this document believe that there is a clear "biblical mandate for sexuality." When the document became public, a number of us on the faculty wrote a brief response, noting that some of us "hear in Scripture a word that is different" from the views expressed in the "Declaration." The conversation has continued in informal discussions, campus publications, and public forums. Now, through this volume, we open our conversations to the larger community of faith, hoping thereby to contribute in some way to the life of the church. The contributors write not merely as scholars and theological educators, but as people who are deeply committed to the church. While it is safe to say that homosexuality is not an area of initial academic interest for any of us, we are *all* persuaded that it is an important issue facing the church today. Whatever our own positions may be, we write because we care about the ministry of the church in the name of Jesus Christ. Some of us began with firm convictions on one or the other side of the issue, but others of us began without knowing where research might lead.

My initial proposal to my faculty colleagues was to produce a volume on "Gender, Sexuality, and Theological Imagination." All members of the faculty were invited to contribute. The response was immediate. Indeed, it was so overwhelming that I have had to limit the topic for now to the issue of homosexuality. Needless to say, the mandate of the 205th General Assembly of the Presbyterian Church (U.S.A.) to study the issue for three years has influenced this decision to focus on homosexuality. My own hope is that other volumes will follow, reflecting the ongoing conversations in this particular community on the topics of gender and theological imagination, as well as on ecumenics and missions. Although the specific subject matters may differ, some of the theological and methodological issues are the same. The fundamental question is how we live out the gospel in our generation.

This book is divided into three parts. In Part 1, "What Do the Scriptures Say?" the primary focus is "exegesis"—the explication of relevant biblical passages. The essays in Part 2, "How Do Scriptures Inform Our Theological Reflection?" consider how the scriptures function in the church as a confessional and liturgical (worshiping) community. These chapters are concerned with "hermeneutics," how we understand the texts to work in our contexts. Part 3 addresses the question "How Do We Live Faithfully?" Here the book focuses on the issues of ethics; the writers are concerned with how a Christian pastor or layperson may come to a decision on the issue at hand. The three-part division is, admittedly, more of a convenient and easily recognizable structure than a methodologically considered one. It is artificial inasmuch as there is some overlap in the issues addressed by the contributors. My point in the organization of the book is, however, that we *must* move beyond the explication of texts. The issue of homosexuality is not merely an exegetical one—that is, it is not merely a question of what the ancient texts *meant*. It is, more importantly, a hermeneutical issue, a question of how we understand the texts and appropriate them for our specific contexts. It is, further, a theological-ethical issue, a question of how we as Christians think about ourselves and our conduct in relation to God.

In the opening chapter, Richard E. Whitaker examines the creation narratives in Genesis 1—3, commonly acknowledged as fundamental texts for the discussion on human sexuality. He makes the point that each of these chapters in Genesis presents creation from a different angle; thus the total picture of creation—including any insights that one might gain on human sexuality—is far richer than the sum of the individual parts. My own contribution in chapter 2, while beginning with an orientation to the Old Testament texts most frequently used in the debate, argues for considering some other texts as well. My thesis is that the wisdom literature of the Bible provides us with a scriptural warrant for paying attention to the contributions of natural and social sciences, and to the testimony of human experience. In chapter 3, Brian K. Blount examines the Pauline passages that make reference to homoerotic sexual activity. He argues that Paul's view on such activities is socially and historically conditioned (as evident in contemporaneous texts from Hellenistic Judaism and the Greco-Roman world); as such, Paul's position on same-sex activity must be distinguished from Paul's "indicative faith pronouncement" that remains a reality for us. Ulrich W. Mauser makes the case in chapter 4 that the issue of homosexuality cannot be isolated from the larger question of human sexuality. He maintains that the New Testament view of sexual ethics is very much shaped by the sexual differentiation of humanity as "male and female" attested to in Genesis.

Patrick D. Miller takes the title of his chapter in Part 2 from the Westminster Shorter Catechism: "What the Scriptures Principally Teach." Miller considers the theological dilemma that Christians face when the "rule of faith" is found to be in tension with "the rule of love." He argues that one must differentiate between what is at the "core" of the Bible—what the scriptures principally teach—and the specifics that each generation of believers must work out for itself. Thomas G. Long reflects in chapter 6 on how the Bible may be read in ordinary congregations struggling to make sense of the vicissitudes of life. Beginning with the particular story of an American family struggling with the death of their gay son, Long ponders how Christians "live" with the Bible. On account of the ambiguities of scripture and the sciences, Mark McClain-Taylor calls into question the popular assumption that homosexuality is a sin. He appeals, instead, for a "theo-ethical hermeneutic of grace and sin," arguing that we must ask whether homosexual practice indeed contravenes the good of what God has done through Jesus Christ. Charles L. Bartow also is interested in how the Bible may be read in the congregation. In light of the confessional standards of the PC(USA), he considers the task of the preacher as servant of the Word. Taking Rom. 1:18–32 as a case in point, Bartow argues in chapter 8 that the rhetorical structure of the passage directs the reader to its theological and emotional content. The preacher is duty-bound to read the text and proclaim the gospel in fidelity to this apostolic testimony. The task of the preacher is also the concern of James F. Kay in chapter 9. He analyzes the arguments of "traditionalist" and "reformist" preachers on the subject of homosexuality. Taking Channing E. Phillips and William Sloane Coffin of the Riverside church as representatives, Kay subjects their sermons to criteria for judging doctrinal faithfulness. He argues that ecclesiastical adjudication about homosexuality must begin within the worshiping community through the preaching of the gospel; it is theologically inappropriate to decide the issue initially as a question of polity.

The pastor, according to Thomas W. Gillespie, faces a dilemma in the issue of homosexuality. On the one hand, the pastor cannot neglect the reality that this issue concerns real human beings, people for whom the pastor may care deeply. On the other hand, the pastor is called to be faithful to the gospel. Gillespie contends that it *is* faithful to tell homosexual people the gospel truth, the good news of Jesus Christ to free people from the oppression of every sin. At the same time, the justice of God revealed in the gospel impels the pastor to seek to overcome "systemic injustice that oppresses human life." In chapter 11, Andrew K. M. Adam locates the basis for Christian sexual ethics in a theological understanding of relationships based upon the character of God's relationship with Jesus, Israel, and the church. In his view, the relationships that are theologically validated, whether heterosexual or homosexual, are characterized by the "constancy" of the partners and not by one's particular sexuality. Max L. Stackhouse, while affirming the need for faithfulness in human relationships, defends the "heterosexual norm" that he finds in the classical Christian tradition. For Stackhouse, God's creative intention is most fully expressed in "[f]aithful, enduring, fertile, marriage bonds," and humanity is created with the freedom to exercise moral will. In the final chapter, Nancy J. Duff argues that it is necessary to seriously consider the arguments of contrary positions, even when there appears to be no moral dilemma—when one is absolutely certain that one is morally right. She then proceeds to model this way of wrestling with moral issues by considering specific arguments against homosexuality as presented in the "Princeton Declaration."

Clearly, the contributors to this volume are not of one mind on the issue of homosexuality. Like our forebears in biblical times, we find ourselves in substantial disagreement. At stake for us all is the gospel: How are we to understand our obligation as a people of faith? We struggle to balance two biblical portrayals of God: a God whose name is Jealous and a God whose name is Compassionate. There are risks that we may err by overemphasizing one or the other divine reality. Yet it is imperative that the church live with this risk and decide what it means to be faithful to the gospel in our day and age.

It gives me great pleasure to thank those who made this volume possible. I begin by acknowledging the dedication of my colleagues who took time from their busy schedules—in some cases interrupting their sabbaticals—to make their contributions. Christine E. R. Yoder, my editorial assistant, provided indispensable help to me at every stage of my work on this book. I want also to thank Stephanie Egnotovich, managing editor at Westminster John Knox Press, for her assistance in the development of this project.

CHOON-LEONG SEOW

Contributors

ANDREW K. M. ADAM is Assistant Professor of New Testament at Princeton Theological Seminary. He is an ordained Episcopal priest.

CHARLES L. BARTOW is the Carl and Helen Egner Professor of Speech Communication in Ministry at Princeton Theological Seminary. He is an ordained minister of the Presbyterian Church (U.S.A.).

BRIAN K. BLOUNT is Assistant Professor of New Testament at Princeton Theological Seminary. He is an ordained minister of the Presbyterian Church (U.S.A.).

NANCY J. DUFF is Associate Professor of Theological Ethics at Princeton Theological Seminary. She is an ordained minister of the Presbyterian Church (U.S.A.).

THOMAS W. GILLESPIE is President of Princeton Theological Seminary and Professor of New Testament. He is an ordained minister of the Presbyterian Church (U.S.A.).

JAMES F. KAY is Associate Professor of Homiletics and Liturgics at Princeton Theological Seminary. He is an ordained minister of the Presbyterian Church (U.S.A.).

THOMAS G. LONG is the Francis Landey Patton Professor of Preaching and Worship at Princeton Theological Seminary. He is an ordained minister of the Presbyterian Church (U.S.A.).

MARK MCCLAIN-TAYLOR is Associate Professor of Theology and Culture at Princeton Theological Seminary. He is an ordained minister of the Presbyterian Church (U.S.A.).

ULRICH W. MAUSER is the Otto A. Piper Professor of Biblical Theology at Princeton Theological Seminary. He is an ordained minister of the Presbyterian Church (U.S.A.).

PATRICK D. MILLER is the Charles T. Haley Professor of Old Testament Theology at Princeton Theological Seminary. He is an ordained minister of the Presbyterian Church (U.S.A.).

CHOON-LEONG SEOW is the Henry Snyder Gehman Professor of Old Testament Language and Literature at Princeton Theological Seminary. He is an ordained elder in the Presbyterian Church (U.S.A.).

MAX L. STACKHOUSE is the Stephen Colwell Professor of Christian Ethics at Princeton Theological Seminary. He is an ordained minister in the United Church of Christ.

RICHARD E. WHITAKER is Information Research Specialist and Lecturer in Old Testament at Princeton Theological Seminary. He is an ordained minister in the United Methodist Church.

Part 1

What Do the Scriptures Say?

1

Creation and Human Sexuality

Richard E. Whitaker

There is no question that the creation accounts in Genesis 1—3 (specifically, in Gen. 1:26–27 and 2:24) are fundamental to the discussion about homosexuality in the church. Most scholars agree that these texts are critical, even though they contain no clear reference to homosexuality. It is important to pay close attention to the larger context of these narratives, that is, Genesis 1—3, as well as to the details and nuances in each of the accounts. The purpose of this chapter is to provide a general background and some guidelines for the interpretation of Genesis 1—3 for the current discussion about human sexuality.

It is admittedly difficult to explicate texts so thoroughly studied and well known. These narrative texts concerning creation have been analyzed frequently by so many interpreters that it is unlikely we will discover anything radically new. The best that we can do is to bring a varied perspective to the text that will, perhaps, enable us to see something we have not considered in the same way before. If these chapters in Genesis presented clear and unambiguous answers concerning human sexuality, the issue of homosexuality in the church would be resolved for many (though not all) Christians. Yet as this is not the case and as scriptures still play a critical role in Christian ethics, we must continue to wrestle with these texts. The questions we bring have no easy answers.

As we look at these narratives, there are several things we need to keep in mind. First, the texts were not written to answer the questions that we may bring to them. Their concern is neither with human sexuality in general nor with homosexuality in particular. Whatever they may say about either topic will be implicit at best, rather than explicit. Second, the texts that we are considering are narratives rather than logical explanations. This does not mean that they are illogical or unclear in their presentation, but rather that the kind of truth and meaning they communicate is different than the kind of truth expressed through logical explanations. Third, the narratives about creation were written neither at the same time nor by the same author. Genesis 1:1–2:4a, for instance, represents one account, whereas Gen. 2:4b–3:24 is a second account, incorporating two perspectives.

My assumption about the texts is that their literary background is sufficiently uncertain that our interpretation should not depend on what specific knowledge we have about authorship, dating of texts, or intended audience. While they may or may not have been parts of earlier documents, there are clear continuities and discontinuities in style, vocabulary, grammatical usage, and story line, such that we may trace "threads" of material elsewhere in Genesis that may help clarify the passages in question. Moreover, the narratives have been collated at some point in their history because, taken together, they convey a meaning that exceeds the sum of their separate meanings.

The accounts in Genesis 1, 2, and 3, although a continuous narrative, consider creation from three fairly distinct perspectives. In Genesis 1, creation is presented in its orderliness; the world moves from day to day and season to season with a predictability that makes planning possible and work rewarding. This world is viewed more as an organism than as a machine and, perhaps, even more as a society than as an organism. Everything that is created is addressed personally, as if it were capable of responding to the Creator: for example, "let the waters under the sky be gathered together into one place" (1:9); "let the waters bring forth swarms of living creatures" (1:20); "let birds fly above the earth across the dome of the sky" (1:20). All that happens in the creative process is described in dynamic terms, as if everything comes to be as a result of will, decision, or obedience, as in Gen. 1:12: "the earth brought forth vegetation." It is, nonetheless, a dependable world; everything happens according to God's word. There are distinctions among the created things of the world, and those distinctions remain unblurred. Humanity is one of the distinct communities that has its place in the created order.

A second perspective on creation appears in Genesis 2, where the relationship within and among various species is emphasized. The created world in this account is conceived from a more "ecological" point of view. The constitutive elements in this ecological environment are intrinsically related. The creatures in this account, unlike those in Genesis 1, occupy particular "niches," but no niche is the exclusive domain of any creature. Creatures differ, but they also share characteristics that transcend the boundaries of specie definitions.

In Genesis 3, creation appears in its ambiguity and unpredictability. The world is a place wherein creatures make unpredictable choices that have predictable consequences. Human decisions have ramifications upon the course of events, not only for those who make the choices, but also for others in the symbiotic environment. Genesis 3 recognizes the ambiguities that exist despite the orderliness of the created world.

These perspectives give a dynamic to the narrative that provides a fuller picture of creation than any one account could convey. We are inclined to think that truth is found in one perspective, but truth may be seen from different angles in a narrative.

How is human sexuality understood in each of these perspectives? What theological and ethical implications might these different angles bring to our discussion on homosexuality?

Creation as the Establishment of Order: Gen. 1:1–2:4a

God is portrayed in Genesis 1 as a sovereign who is ordering the universe, much like the god Marduk in the Babylonian creation account known as the *Enuma Elish*.[1] In the latter account, Marduk's power as a warrior is emphasized and his right to sovereignty is achieved in his victory over the chaotic waters—deified in the person of Tiamat ("Deep")—that are the stuff of creation. Marduk splits these waters to form the cosmos. Unlike the Babylonian epic, however, the focus of Genesis 1 is not on victory in combat over the forces of chaos but on the orderliness of creation and its procreational ability. In the orderliness of the world, one finds witness to God's sovereignty, a sovereignty not threatened by the nature of the chaos that exists. God needs no victory to assure dominion. God merely speaks, and chaos is ordered. For the further ordering of the world, God then calls into existence Light, which distinguishes day from night (Gen. 1:3–5), and Firmament, which distinguishes "the waters from the waters" (Gen. 1:6–7). Thus, the ordering of creation is evident in the structure of heaven and earth in the midst of the waters (according to ancient Near Eastern cosmology), in the division of time into days, seasons, and years, and in the classification of creatures into species. It is within this last "ordering" that the creation of humankind is included.

The specificity of the species is indicated by the language of the text: "of every kind" (vv. 11, 12, 21 [twice], 24 [twice], 25 [thrice]). Moreover, plants, birds and other creatures perpetuate themselves within their own species: "plants yielding seed, and fruit trees of every kind on earth that bear fruit with the seed in it" (vv. 11, 12; see also vv. 21, 22, 24, 25). As for the "living creatures," they are blessed and commanded to "be fruitful and multiply" (v. 22).

The resulting world is self-sustaining, procreative, and orderly. The firmament continues to separate the waters above from the waters below. The luminaries (sun, moon, and stars) continue to rule over the day and night and mark times and seasons. The earth continues to sprout forth vegetation, while the seas swarm with living creatures. The animals and birds continue to be fruitful, to multiply, and to fill the earth and sky. The sovereign God does not have to look after every detail in order to maintain sovereignty, although the direct activity of God in the details of the created world is not precluded.

Humankind, contrary to the animals, is created in "the image and likeness" of God (Gen. 1:26). The exact meaning of this is not explicitly stated. Because humanity is referred to in this context as "male and female" (Gen. 1:27), some interpreters have understood the sociality or sexuality of humanity to be the "image of God." This is, however, unlikely. The terminology of "male and female" identifies distinctions within humankind as biological creatures. Similarly, the categories of "male and female" are used in reference to animals preserved in Noah's ark for the reproduction of their "kinds" after the flood (Gen. 6:19; 7:3, 8, 16). In fact, "male and female" is used exclusively of animals except here in Genesis 1 and in the reference to this act of the creation of humanity (Gen. 5:2). While sexual distinction is not, therefore, unique to humans, the "image of God" clearly is. There is no indication whatsoever that sexual distinction is a part of the divine character.

The only thing that clearly distinguishes humanity from the other species is that humanity has dominion over all of the other creatures. If there is anything in this passage that tells us what the "image of God" is for humanity, it would have to be this dominion. In any case, humankind as "male" and "female" is, on the one hand, a specie like other species of animals. On the other hand, humankind is unlike any other specie insofar as it (both male and female) is the "image of God." As humanity is created in the "image and likeness" of God, it is not necessary for the divine sovereign to be constantly present in order for dominion to be maintained in the created world. Humanity represents God in exercising that dominion over the other creatures. Therefore, on the seventh day—the day after the creation of humankind—the sovereign God rested from the labors of creation.

Genesis 1 identifies only two sexes that are involved in the definition of humanity in its entirety and in its role as a reproductive specie. Genesis 1 offers no grounds for excluding any human being, regardless of sex or sexual orientation, because sexuality is not what defines the "image of God." Further, the text offers no perspective from which to consider homosexual males or females as other than males and females.

Howard Eilberg-Schwartz has argued that the Levitical laws should be read in light of Genesis 1.[2] If so, the assumptions and functions of Levitical law may be more clearly understood. The orderliness and procreative nature of creation obligated human beings to act in a manner that sustained order and procreativity. With regard to questions of sexuality, the laws forbidding sexual relations between humans and animals (Lev. 18:23) and homosexual relations (Lev. 18:22) are directly linked to this understanding of the order, the specificity of the species, and the procreative nature of creation. But, as Eilberg-Schwartz notes, "Israel is not merely expected to imitate God. Israel is also expected to reaffirm and uphold the distinctions God implanted in the world at creation."[3] The purpose of sexual distinction, therefore, is procreation—the maintenance of the specie over time. Even the terminology for the homosexual act, "lying with a male as one lies with a woman," reflects this understanding that sex is intended to be between a male and a female.

Creation as the Establishment of Relationship: Gen. 2:4b–25

The creation account in Gen. 2:4b–25 opens with a concern for the productivity of the earth "when no plant of the field was yet in the earth and no herb of the field had yet sprung up" (2:5). Unlike the imperative to "be fruitful and multiply" in Genesis 1, however, the angle here does not focus on the species of plants and their ability to reproduce their own kind. It is, rather, on providing the means by which the plants can flourish—watering and tilling (Gen. 2:5–6). When all of the elements necessary for flourishing are in place, the result is termed a "garden" (2:8–9). God planted a garden in which to put the creature '$\bar{a}d\bar{a}m$. It is difficult to know whether to translate the Hebrew term '$\bar{a}d\bar{a}m$ as "man" or "humankind" within this context. When "Woman" is created, she originates from the same creature and is separated off to become a corresponding being; the original '$\bar{a}d\bar{a}m$ is the source of both "man" and "woman." The term used to refer to the original creature ('$\bar{a}d\bar{a}m$) continues to be, however, the term used for the "man" ('$\bar{a}d\bar{a}m$), as distinguished from the "woman." In any case, it should be noted that it is " '$\bar{a}d\bar{a}m$," not God, who makes the judgment that "this one" is acceptable.

The concern within the narrative is to suggest why the '$\bar{a}d\bar{a}m$ needs to have a human "helper" (2:18): Nonhuman creatures would not do. Carol Meyers has argued convincingly that the "helper" term is not to be read as subordinating the helper to the one helped.[4] Although not explicitly stated, the text suggests that the woman is to be seen as a companion, a coworker, and a partner in sexual reproduction. The role of the woman as companion is indicated by God's proclamation that "it is not good for the '$\bar{a}d\bar{a}m$ to be alone" (2:18, author's trans.). It is also possible that the need for companionship was occasioned by the human responsibility to till and to keep the garden, a responsibility suggested by the verse that states "there was no one to till the ground" (2:5). This is consistent with the fact that what is sought for the '$\bar{a}d\bar{a}m$ is a "helper," a companion worker in the garden. Finally, the woman's role as a partner in sexual reproduction is implied in the passage, insofar as "a man leaves his father and his mother and clings to his wife, and they become one flesh" (2:24).

It is evident in the text, then, that the relationships between creatures, here the male and female of humanity, are dynamic and complex. Sex and sexual reproduction are not fully definitive of humanity's identity and role in the created order. Such complexity of relationships is further the case between humanity and its environment. The '*ādām*, as both man and woman, tills and keeps the garden, but '*ādām* is not simply its caretaker. Man and woman are also to delight in the trees that are "pleasant to the sight" and to enjoy the fruits that are "good for food" (2:9). There is a mutual benefit, a symbiosis, between humankind and the environment. They need each other. God allows the flourishing of this environment to depend upon humanity. At the same time, the nourishment and pleasure of humanity depends, at least in part, on the garden. Only the tree of the knowledge of good and evil is excluded by God's command from this symbiotic relationship. This tree is not intended for the use of humankind; it is not clear whether they are to tend to it. Even so, it is up to humankind to obey God's intention that they do not partake of its fruit or touch it.

The relation of the human to the animals, second, involves both a likeness and a difference. The animals are, like humans, living beings. While they were formed from the ground, as was the human, the text does not specify that God breathed into them to enliven them as God did with the human. God brought each of the animals to the '*ādām* to see what the '*ādām* would name it. The text introduces a new element here that goes beyond Genesis 1: human freedom. The absolute, orderly distinctions between species in Genesis 1 are not emphasized here. The '*ādām* names the animals and, thereby, classifies them. God allows the human the freedom of decision and action, apparently without compromising divine sovereignty. It becomes clear, however, that no suitable "helper" for the '*ādām* would come from among the animals. Apart from the fact that both humans and animals get their food from plants, nothing more is said of their relationship to each other.

Thus, in Gen. 2:4b–25, the various roles of plants and animals help to define the relationships enjoyed by humanity. As man and woman till and keep the garden, they enjoy the fruits of their labors; as they name the animals, they exercise their God-given freedom to make distinctions. It is the assumption of the story that humanity labors, rejoices, and makes decisions in relationship to each other and to their environment. Clearly, the "man" and the "woman" are of different sexes and will be drawn together closely by a sexual bond (see 2:24) but at this point, human sexuality is a secondary concern to relationship. The contention of some interpreters that Gen. 2:24 (with its possible allusion to marriage) is not original to the story may or may not be true. In any case, the verse does anticipate something that is important for the relationship of the man and woman in Genesis 3.

While the Levitical laws introduce imperatives to maintain and support the order that God has created, Genesis 2 presents that very order as having some dependency upon human beings as well. It is not just that the world is self-sustaining. The ideal world, if that term is appropriate, is a world in which human responses are consistent with the ordering of creation. The nature of that ordering is not predetermined by God; rather, God defines only the boundaries within which humans may function. Only God could create the animals, yet it is the human who names them. As for sexuality, it involves the sharing of tasks and the enjoyment together of the fruits of labor. It may be observed that when the '$\bar{a}d\bar{a}m$ saw the woman, what he recognized was not a sexually differentiated creature, but someone just like himself; she is his "own bone," his "very flesh" (author's trans.).

Creation as Unpredictable: Genesis 3

Genesis 3 is clearly a continuation of the narrative in Genesis 2. It has none of the literary discontinuities that we find between Genesis 1 and Genesis 2. Yet there is sufficient change in the situation to warrant an analysis of its distinct contribution. Humanity is placed in a new relationship with creation; it is a relationship in which all is not as it should be.

This narrative, which recounts how the first couple was expelled from the garden, makes no reference to their sexuality. In the *Gilgamesh Epic* from Mesopotamia, there is an account of how Enkidu, the friend of Gilgamesh, loses his relationship with his animal companions as a consequence of having had sex with a prostitute.[5] This tempting parallel has led some interpreters to contend that the "knowledge of good and evil" is, in fact, human knowledge of sexuality. This is a particularly attractive interpretation given that the immediate result of the man and the woman eating the fruit was their awareness of their nakedness. But the act in which they became aware, unlike the act of Enkidu, was not itself a sexual act.

There are sufficient treatments of this narrative exploring possible reasons for the expulsion from the garden. I will consider only the nature of that expulsion. The punishment of the serpent is apparently based on its own action, not that of the man and the woman. Nevertheless, the result of the serpent's temptation of the woman is future enmity between humankind and the serpent. When the man and woman eat the fruit, they become aware of their nakedness and feel such shame that they hide themselves. In this, like Enkidu of the *Gilgamesh Epic*, they are further distinguished from the animals who have no shame in their nakedness.

The punishment of the man involves his responsibility as a tiller and keeper of the ground, not his sexuality. The ground, which is dependent upon cultivation for its fruitfulness, is cursed: Humanity is no longer assured of its fertility. This curse accounts for the subsequent ineffectiveness of the man as a tiller. Not only does the earth no longer respond to his tilling as it did in the past, but tilling becomes a painful toil. The symbiosis is not broken, but it is very much compromised.

Unlike the punishment of the man, the punishment of the woman concerns her sexual role as a childbearer. Not since Genesis 1 have we had any mention of humans as reproductive beings. It is only here, in anticipation of their expulsion from the garden as mortals, that the woman is told she will bear children through a painful process. I cannot accept Carol Meyers's attempt to interpret the pain of the woman specifically as a reference to the strain of raising children and not to the pain of childbearing. To be sure, the reference to the woman's desire for her husband and to his ruling over her may both be related to the process of childbearing.[6] Apparently, the man shall have the right to overrule the woman when it comes to the question of whether they shall have children. Yet we should continue to see the whole verse as concerned with the woman's role as childbearer. The text, in any case, is not to be interpreted as a granting of general dominion to men.

The consequences faced by the man and the woman are consistent with the punishment stipulated for eating of the fruit of the tree of knowledge: "You shall surely die" (Gen. 3:3). In short, they become mortal. The expulsion from the garden is a guarantee that they will not be able to overcome this mortality. The effects of mortality upon humankind as tillers and as procreative beings are profound. They will die without food and they will cease to exist as a specie without procreation. The choices that they make with regard to their labor to produce food and their procreation will effect not only themselves, but other people, the land, and other creatures. Today we realize how this is true in ways that the ancient Israelites never could have fathomed.

Two Sexual Models: Genesis 1—3

We have come full circle from sexuality as the procreative relationship between the male and female (Genesis 1) to sexuality as the procreative relationship between man and woman (Genesis 3). There is a difference, however, in what sexuality means in each of these accounts. In the first (Genesis 1), sexuality is part of the order of the world; it is the means by which humans, like all other creatures, take their place as a specie in a self-sustaining world. They are the image (reflection) of the sovereign God in the earthly realm. In the second (Genesis 3), procreation is a necessity forced upon humanity by the reality of death; it is the means of preserving the specie in the face of mortality. Sexuality implies companionship, sharing of tasks, and the enjoyment of each other and of the environment. But those possibilities are necessarily subordinated to the fact that humans die, and only painful labor and procreation will preserve the specie.

Where Do We Go from Here?

The general context for the creation narratives (Genesis 1—3) is sufficiently clear. These accounts are addressed to people struggling to find order in a world that will ensure their continued existence and that of the other species. Even though existing order makes life dependable and planning practical, humans make many choices that radically affect how that order operates—even, perhaps, to the point of near chaos. Often, choices are made before their implications are fully understood.

A basic part of our ethical decision-making is to act in accordance with the discernible order that God has created in the world. This is indeed true in the area of sexual ethics. We are inclined to talk about sexuality in terms of doing what is "natural." This concept of what is natural has remained the basis for the rejection of any form of sexual activity that lies outside the pattern of procreative sex between a human male and a human female. In the context of the creation accounts in Genesis 2 and 3, however, this sexual relationship occurs between people who share a cooperative bond of companionship and commitment. Those who seek justification for homosexual patterns of relationship often base their justification on arguments that the homosexual person is by nature homosexual or, indeed, that there are several sexual patterns that are natural other than that of the heterosexual male and female. To make this case, however, one must look beyond these creation accounts for evidence that homosexuality is a part of the created order. The creation material in Genesis 1—3 accepts, or at least assumes, that procreation is the primary purpose of human sexual relationships.

Such an approach to sexual ethics is open to reexamination in two areas. The first is whether the procreational model is sufficient for understanding sexual naturalness in creation. The views of sexuality in Genesis 2 seem more pertinent today than those of Genesis 1 or 3. Sexuality as companionship, as the sharing of tasks, as the enjoying together of the fruits of our labors and of each other, fits easily into contemporary society. In many families these dynamics of relationships take precedence over procreation. Few people today, for instance, would argue that childless couples share an "unnatural" relationship. Even fewer would consider it unnatural for couples who are beyond the childbearing age to have sexual relations. What are our reasons for insisting that in all families the partners must be of opposite sexes? If we accept or endorse other patterns of sexuality, do we somehow undermine the created goodness of heterosexual relationships?

Must the sexual distinctions between humans have a primary function of reproduction? It remains true that we are always only one generation away from extinction. If we cease to reproduce, we cease to exist. But the danger of extinction faced in antiquity due to shortage of labor and resources is no longer a serious threat. Our danger comes from overpopulation, not underpopulation. We still need the primary social institutions that support procreation; none of our experiments with substitutes for the family as a child-rearing institution have proven successful. It is no longer necessary, however, to see every primary social institution solely as a context for pro-creation.

The second area for reexamination is closely related. Some of the assumptions at work in the Genesis creation accounts, particularly as they inform the Levitical laws, are based on upholding distinctions in the created world. We understand the maintenance of order and divisions within the physical world differently today. For example, whereas in the ancient agricultural system it may have been advantageous to maintain the purity of strains of grain and cattle, the modern system of agriculture depends upon hybridization and selective cross-breeding. Moreover, in antiquity people assumed that the species had always existed as they were. We, however, are aware of the ever-changing character of the natural world and of the indefinite character of specie boundaries. Few of our garments today are made from only one material. How many of the "natural" distinctions that were made in antiquity must we maintain? Genesis 1 is concerned with the orderliness of creation and the distinctions that *God* has made, including the classification of species of plants, birds, animals, and humanity. It is in this context that one is told of the difference between male and female. Genesis 1 is, however, silent about the role and ability of human beings in God's order. By contrast, in Genesis 2, the focus shifts to human freedom and ability to make distinctions and choices. Genesis 1 emphasizes God's sovereign power; Genesis 2 highlights human freedom. How do we balance these two perspectives on creation in a manner that takes seriously the contribution of each? Does Genesis 2 allow us, human beings who are free to name and to distinguish, to identify categories that are not explicitly mentioned in Genesis 1? If humanity's naming is not limited to the definitions made in Genesis 1, are we permitted to name alternate or additional identities besides "male and female"?

The distinction between male and female may not be the only one that can be made. And if we do not limit ourselves to these particular definitions, might we discover that distinctions within humanity can be made along a variety of lines? Do these choices have consequences we cannot predict or imagine? Or is God still expecting us to bear the responsibility of naming, the responsibility of what kind of garden we will make of the world?

The fruit of the tree of the knowledge of good and evil was just like the fruit of every other tree in the garden. It was good to look at and desirable to eat. The woman and the man had even been told which tree it was. Outside that garden, where we must make significant choices and bear important responsibilities, however, the trees all look alike. It is a place where there are uncertainties and risks. Nevertheless, it is here that we stand; we can do no other.

NOTES

1. James B. Pritchard, ed., *Ancient Near Eastern Texts Relating to the Old Testament*, 3d ed. with supplements (Princeton: Princeton University Press, 1969), 60–72.
2. Howard Eilberg-Schwartz, "Creation and Classification in Judaism: From Priestly to Rabbinic Conceptions," *History of Religion* 26 (1987): 361.
3. Ibid., 362.
4. Carol Meyers, *Discovering Eve: Ancient Israelite Women in Context* (New York: Oxford University Press, 1988), 85.
5. J. Pritchard, *Ancient Near Eastern Texts*, 72–99.
6. C. Meyers, *Discovering Eve*, 95–109.

2

A Heterotextual Perspective

Choon-Leong Seow

Very few texts in the Old Testament, indeed in the Bible as a whole, explicitly address the issue of same-sex intercourse. Within the Old Testament, interpreters frequently cite the prohibition in Leviticus (18:22; 20:13), the story about the destruction of Sodom and Gomorrah (Gen. 19:1–38) and a related account of rape in Judg. 19:1–30. Beyond these, however, it is common to appeal to the creation accounts in Genesis, as well as to theological models for human relationships, such as the conjugal imageries and metaphors that are scattered throughout the Bible. The purpose of this chapter is to provide the reader with a textual orientation—an orientation to the Old Testament texts that have commonly been cited—and then to consider the possibility of looking beyond the standard texts to an often neglected portion of the Bible, namely, the wisdom literature.

Legal and Narrative Passages

The most explicit texts in the Old Testament concerning same-sex activity come from the so-called Holiness Code in Leviticus 17—26. This is the only place in all the Bible where we find clear injunctions against same-sex acts: "You shall not lie with a male as with a woman; it is an abomination" (Lev. 18:22); "If a man lies with a male as with a woman, both of them have committed an abomination; they shall be put to death, their blood is upon them" (Lev. 20:13). In terms of what the texts *say*, there can be absolutely no doubt. Same-sex intercourse between males is prohibited.[1] There is also no question that an "abomination" (*tôʻēbâ*) is anything that is unacceptable in Israelite culture; the Hebrew word (*tôʻēbâ*) may be used of unclean food (Deut. 14:3), idols (2 Kings 23:13; Isa. 44:19), idolatrous practices (Deut. 12:31; 13:15), child sacrifice (Deut. 12:31), remarriage of divorced women (Deut. 24:4), magic (Deut. 18:12), marrying outside the faith-community (Mal. 2:11), the prayer of those who do not obey the law (Prov. 28:9), and so forth. For many Christians, it is as simple as that: If these biblical texts *say* homosexual acts are forbidden, then homosexuality cannot be acceptable. People who are openly homosexual, therefore, cannot be ordained to the ministry.

Yet difficult problems are encountered in appealing to these prohibitions. The text is clear that homosexual acts between men are an abomination, but it is equally clear that remarriage of a woman after divorce is an abomination (Deut. 24:4). Why should one stipulation be considered valid and the other not? Why should the prohibition of same-sex intercourse be normative today, but not the stipulated death penalty? Why should this prohibition (against male-male homoerotic acts) be applicable but not others in the same Holiness Code, like the crossbreeding of animals, the mixing of grain or fiber, various dietary regulations, and so forth? The Holiness Code is equally clear that children who slight their parents should be put to death (Lev. 20:9).[2] Why should we not apply that law today? As for the qualifications for the ordained ministry, the portion of the Holiness Code that seems most pertinent are those laws regarding the priesthood (Lev. 21:1–24). Priests should not trim their sideburns or their beards, nor should they marry non-virgins, widows, or divorcees. They must only marry within their own clan. They should not be blind or lame, have a limb too long or too short, have an impaired leg or an impaired hand, be hunchbacked, be too thin or small, have defective eyesight, have a festering rash or some other skin disease, or have damaged testicles. Indeed, they are disqualified if they have any physical defects whatsoever! So how do we decide that these regulations that are explicitly concerned with ordination to the ministry are not relevant today, but the prohibitions about homosexual acts are? All these texts are clear in terms of what they actually *say*. Yet we must recognize that they are culturally conditioned and cannot be applied uncritically.

Perhaps more than the Holiness Code, many Christians think of the story of the destruction of Sodom and Gomorrah in Genesis 19 as a text clearly indicating the wickedness of same-sex activity. It is evident, however, that the narrative is not about same-sex love. Rather, it is a story about wickedness in general, violence, and the violation of a sacrosanct code of hospitality.[3] Gang rape is at issue in the passage, not same-sex love. Indeed, Sodom and Gomorrah appear many more times in the Old Testament, but the problem is never the homoeroticism of the offense. Apart from general references to the wickedness of the cities, the traditions speak of injustice, sin of adultery, lies, pride, gluttony, excess wealth, indifference to the poor, and their inhospitality (Isa. 1:10; 3:9; Jer. 23:14; Ezek. 16:49; Wisd. Sol. 19:14–15; Matt. 10:12–15; Luke 10:12–12). Not once in the Bible is homoeroticism given as the reason for the annihilation of the cities. It is true that Jude 7 suggests that sex is an issue, but the point in Jude is not same-sex intercourse. Rather it is that mortals have transgressed the boundaries between human and celestial beings. Curiously the offense, according to Jude, is that mortals have gone after "other flesh" (Greek, *sarkos heteras*). Strictly speaking, the problem in Jude is not that these offenders were *homosexual* but that their desires were overly *heterosexual*—so much so that they were going after "other" (that is, non-human) bodies. In any case, all that one can extract from Genesis 19 is that the people of Sodom intended to commit gang rape. The fact that the ruffians might have had same-sex rape in mind is irrelevant to our discussion of the acceptability of same-sex love. If homosexual gang rape proves that same-sex love is wrong, then heterosexual rape and adultery must also be said to show that heterosexual love is wrong.

Judges 19 is also commonly cited as a narrative illustration of the wrongness of homosexual acts. There, again, the issue is not same-sex love but gang rape. In fact, the violence that was actually perpetrated was not homosexual but heterosexual. The eventual victim was a woman.[4]

In sum, the passages that either clearly mention or possibly allude to same-sex intercourse are difficult to use in Christian ethics. The only explicit prohibition is embedded in a body of legal materials that are culturally conditioned. The church no longer accepts as authoritative for Christian conduct many regulations that are found in the Levitical instructions. We are inclined to distinguish between "moral" and "ritual" laws, but the labels are arbitrarily applied and foreign to Hebrew thought. For the ancient Israelites, there was no distinction between cultic and moral purity. As for the two narrative passages (Genesis 19 and Judges 19), they are not about same-sex love, but about violence and general wickedness. Here, too, the culturally conditioned character of the biblical narratives must be recognized. Moreover, the narratives reflect ethics that cannot be normative for our times, such as the secondary valuation of women and the offering of one's own kin to ensure that strangers are protected from sexual abuse.

Models for Human Relationships

Some interpreters attempt to provide theological models in the discussion of human sexuality. The texts cited in this approach are not specifically related to same-sex erotic acts, but they are believed to show that heterosexual unions are normative.

Occasionally, an analogy is drawn between human bonds and God's covenant relationship with Israel or the church. In this connection, some have called attention to "the nuptial imagery in Hosea."[5] In this view, it is significant that the book of Hosea, which contains a parable of God's covenantal bond with humanity, portrays marriage as a heterosexual one. Yet the book is conveyed through some images and metaphors that are very difficult for many of us. Commentators have traditionally been troubled by God's command to Hosea to marry a prostitute. More seriously, there are images of domestic violence, which surely cannot be held as normative. So we hear in Hos. 2:3–5 the threat of the husband (God) to punish his wife (Israel):

I will strip her naked,
and expose her as on the day she was born,
I will make her like a wilderness,
and turn her into parched land,
and kill her with thirst.
Upon her children I will have no pity,
because they are children of whoredom.
For their mother has acted as a whore;
she who has conceived them has acted shamefully.

This is clearly not an image of conjugal bliss, heterosexual though the marital relationship is. It can hardly be held as a model for human relationships. The book of Hosea comes to us through culturally conditioned language and metaphors. We are compelled, therefore, to recognize the limitations of the metaphor, even as one affirms the good news of God's persistent love. Fidelity—God's abiding love—is the issue in Hosea. Faithfulness and love are the message that we are supposed to learn from the imagery, not heterosexuality. The book does not provide an appropriate analogy for social relationships.

General references to marriages in the Bible are inadequate, too. While one may point to the model of heterosexuality in typical Israelite marriages, one might demur to the other aspects of Israelite culture, such as polygyny, concubinage, and levirate marriages. Such models are hardly adequate for Christian ethics.

For many interpreters, the first creation account in Genesis 1 is critical in the debate; the Levitical laws presume it, as do most New Testament passages pertaining to human sexuality. Even though the text does not mention homosexual acts, this passage is considered pivotal because it presumes a heterosexual norm: God created humankind as male and female and commanded them to "be fruitful and multiply." So it is argued that heterosexuality was part of God's intention in creation and that heterosexual marriage is normative for humankind. Marriage does not appear to be at issue in the passage, however. Rather, the text is concerned with the orderliness of creation and, specifically, with the reproduction of plants and animals, each "according to its kind" (Gen. 1:11–13; 20–25).[6] So the animals and birds are commanded to reproduce: "be fruitful and multiply" (Gen. 1:22). Then, at the climax of creation, humankind was made in the image of God and also told, like the animals, to "be fruitful and multiply."

It is important to observe that human beings are at once like and unlike God; they are also like and unlike the animals. Here one may detect a subtle polemic against other creation accounts in the ancient Near East. The

Babylonian epic known as *Enuma Elish*, for instance, depicts human beings as a servant-class created merely to serve the whims and fancies of the gods.[7] In contrast to that perspective, the biblical writer of Genesis 1 suggests that human beings, unlike the animals, are created in the image of God—probably meaning that they, like God, have dominion on earth. In Mesopotamia, the presence of the gods was represented by the presence of images (Akkadian *ṣalmu*); in Israelite theology, God's presence on earth is represented by a humanity made in God's image (Hebrew *ṣelem*). Human beings thus represent God's presence on earth in that they exercise dominion. At the same time, humanity is unlike God in that people are sexually differentiated creatures. In this they are like the animals, who are also created as "male and female" (see Gen. 6:19; 7:3, 9, 16; Lev. 3:1, 6; Deut. 4:16). In this differentiation they are unlike God, who is not "male and female." Significantly in this account, human beings are not characterized as "husband and wife" or even "man and woman." Instead of social terms like these, the author uses biological terms: "male and female." They are, thus, like the animals. And just as the animals are commanded to reproduce, so human beings are commanded to "be fruitful and multiply." Here again, the biblical writer may be responding to Babylonian theology, as reflected in the Atraḫasis Epic. Whereas the gods in the Babylonian account have every intention of putting limits on the growth of human population—through drought, pestilence, famine, infertility, and flood, and so on—the biblical perspective emphasizes the very opposite to be the intention of Israel's God: God intends for humanity to "be fruitful and multiply."[8] Contrary to the destructive intentions of the gods in the Atraḫasis Epic, God promised the Israelites: "In your land women will neither miscarry nor be barren" (Ex. 23:26). The intent of the author of Genesis 1 is to affirm the growth of human population.[9] Of the various statements and commands in Genesis 1, it is the command to "be fruitful and multiply" that is reiterated in the narrative history that follows (Gen. 9:1, 7; see also Gen. 8:17; 17:6, 20; 28:3; 48:4; Ex. 1:7; Lev. 26:9). Theologically, one recognizes that the point is the goodness of procreation, and this, too, we must affirm in the church. It is good for humanity to procreate.

Genesis does not tell the full story of creation, however. There are exceptions of which the texts do not speak. It is true that God created humanity as male and female, but we also know there are people who are created as *neither* biologically male nor female, or *both* as male and female. It is true that humanity is, as a rule, created whole and fully able, but it is a reality that there are people who are not born that way. We affirm that mortals are supposed to procreate, but we recognize at the same time that many people are biologically incapable of bearing children. Neither heterosexuality nor the ability to procreate should be held as essential elements in our being human. Surely one ought not argue on the basis of this account that sex is only for the purpose of procreation or that it is unacceptable for people not to be married. We must affirm what is good about creation as we know them from the Genesis accounts, including heterosexuality and procreation, but affirming the goodness of these things does not require us to deny the possibility of other realities that may also be good.

The Wisdom Tradition

Not all truths about creation are recorded in Genesis. Indeed, the scriptures do not reveal all the realities of creation and of life. There are many truths that people may discern from observation of life and the world, and there are realities that may yet remain beyond human comprehension. This is the premise of the Old Testament's wisdom tradition, best represented in the Protestant canon by the books of Proverbs, Job, and Ecclesiastes.

The wisdom tradition emphasizes at once the possibilities and the limitations of knowledge through the observation of nature and human experiences. As Gerhard von Rad defines it, wisdom is "a practical knowledge of the laws of life and of the world, based upon experience . . . [and] the characteristic of practically all that it says about life is this starting point in experience."[10] In this biblical perspective, one does not begin instruction with revelation from on high; there is no "thus saith the LORD" formula in the wisdom books. Wisdom does not focus on the authoritative traditions, either. Noticeably absent from the wisdom texts of Proverbs, Job, and Ecclesiastes are the main themes that one finds elsewhere in the Bible. There is no reference to the promise of God to the ancestors, the liberation of people from bondage, the giving of the law at Sinai, the providence of God in the wilderness wanderings, or the entry into the promised land. In this corpus of biblical literature, one finds no mention of and no allusion to salvation history or the covenant—themes that theologians say are central in the Old Testament. Indeed, some detect in the wisdom tradition a certain reticence in explaining the realities of the world in strict terms of divine cause and effect.

In most of the Bible, events are typically explained in terms of God's direct intervention in history. God brings blessings or curses upon people because of choices that they make; God rewards the obedient, but punishes the wicked. The doctrine of retribution is also present in the wisdom tradition, but in the sages' formulation of it, God is not explicitly involved.[11] For instance, one finds the following saying in Prov. 26:27–28:

Whoever digs a pit will fall into it;
a stone will come back on the one who starts it rolling.
A lying tongue hates its victims,
and a flattering mouth works ruin.

One notices that there is no mention of God here. The one who digs the pit falls into it, the rolled stone rolls itself back, the flattering mouth itself works ruins. People who set traps for others will get caught in their own traps. People who lie may end up hurting themselves. Evil brings evil, good brings good. People reap what they sow. Thus, the consequences follow the acts as if by some law of nature.

The difference in the perspectives between the wisdom tradition and other parts of the Bible is also evident when one compares an injunction against frivolous vows stated in Ecclesiastes with one stated in Deuteronomy. In Ecclesiastes one reads, "When you make a vow to God, do not be slack to fulfill it, for there is no delight in fools" (Eccl. 5:3). The same injunction is found in Deuteronomy, but in the Deuteronomic formulation of the injunction God is clearly named: "When you make a vow to YHWH your God, do not be slack in fulfilling it; for YHWH your God will certainly require it of you and it shall be an offence against you [if you do not fulfill it]" (Deut. 23:21, author's trans.). By contrast, Ecclesiastes states the consequence of unfulfilled vows without explicit reference to the deity: "for there is no delight in fools." By recourse to circumlocution, Ecclesiastes avoids attributing to God the consequences of human conduct. People bring disaster upon themselves by what they do. Period. God may or may not be involved.

It is not that the sages want to deny the possibility of God's involvement in human affairs. The fact is that people need not and must not explain all matters in terms of divine causality. Sometimes there are natural explanations that reason may discover. Sometimes there is no explanation at all. Because of its reluctance to implicate God in all human experiences, the wisdom tradition is sometimes called "secular." Yet it may be argued that wisdom's reticence in using theological language to explain every human experience may itself be a theological posture. God in the wisdom tradition is indeed Creator, but God is not the cause of every effect.

Wisdom's interest in natural explanations most closely resembles what one might call the scientific approach to reality. Wisdom is interested in what is natural, and it does not define what is natural or unnatural by what traditions say. It calls on people to investigate—study the natural and social sciences, as it were. So it is that Solomon, the consummate sage in the Old Testament, "spoke of trees, from the cedar that is in Lebanon to the hyssop that grows out of the wall; he spoke of beasts, and of birds, and of reptiles and of fish" (1 Kings 4:32–33). In a late wisdom text, the sage's activity is said to have included astronomy, zoology, and botany (Wisd. Sol. 7:17–22). In Ben Sira, physicians and pharmacists are extolled as experts whose skills are created by God for humanity's well-being (Sir. 38:1–15).[12] The wisdom literature may be regarded as the Bible's department of "practical theology," a theology that begins with humanity and the realities of the world and not with dogma.

The wisdom tradition of the Bible recognizes that there are truths that do not come by special revelation.[13] The result is neither a systematic theology nor a consistent set of laws. Rather, what the wisdom tradition produces is a series of practical admonitions and general guidelines on how to cope with the vicissitudes of life, although the sages themselves readily admit that those rules are not absolute. They know, too, that because of life's many contradictions, the rules may be contradictory. So we sometimes find conflicting admonitions placed side by side:

> Do not answer fools according to their folly,
> or you will be a fool yourself.
> Answer fools according to their folly,
> or they may be wise in their own eyes.
> (Prov. 26:4–5)

Here we see that the advice to answer fools is juxtaposed with another that says not to answer them. There is no attempt to resolve the contradictions. Unlike modern western thinkers, the sages of Israel see no need to resolve the contradictory advice. Presumably in some situations one proverb works better than the other, but both are equally true. It is not that there is a point, a counterpoint, and finally a resolution, or a thesis, an antithesis, and then a synthesis. Indeed, as scholar Walter J. Harrelson puts it, "wisdom operates without the necessity of a synthesis."[14] This is the way of the wisdom tradition, for it is concerned with the efforts of human beings to cope with life in all its complexities. There are no fail-safe rules, no formula that works every time. So the sages frequently set forth only what is relatively good, often in the form of "Better-than" proverbs (e.g., "Better is open rebuke than hidden love," Prov. 27:5).[15]

The sages know full well the limitations of human wisdom. They recognize that people may be mistaken in what they see and that the experience of one individual cannot be normative for all. Yet they recognize that human observations and experiences are reliable enough that they must not be dismissed too quickly. Human knowledge, though limited, may generally be trusted.[16] The sages know that there are no fail-safe rules—neither those that were thought to have been revealed, not those that the sages have propounded on the basis of observation and experience. Nevertheless, they trust human beings enough not to ignore their voices of experience and doubt.

Here in the Bible, then, one finds the recognition that one can learn truth from what we call natural and social sciences. Humans can learn truths apart from special revelation. Thus, as W. Sibley Towner argues, the wisdom literature of the Bible provides us with a "biblically warranted, theologically validated affirmation of our 'secular' interpretation of experience, comprehended within a theological framework built upon a doctrine of creation as the good handiwork of a creator who remains also sustainer and the ultimate redeemer of the world."[17] Here in the wisdom tradition of the Bible is *scriptural authority* for human beings to make ethical decisions by paying attention to science and human experiences.[18] We must not say, as we often hear in the debate about homosexuality, that "experience has nothing to do with it" or that "only scripture matters." It is scriptural to take human observations and experiences seriously.

This does not mean that we should reject the authoritative traditions and turn only to the sciences and human experience. My point, rather, is that we may not be faithful when we simply hold on to dogmatic statements when the realities of life contradict dogma. Sometimes we have to change, or at least nuance, our long-held positions in the face of new realities. Indeed, Israel's faith survived precisely because of the willingness of its theologians to constantly rethink, even to challenge, the traditions. So it was in the face of the painful experience of exile and destruction, for instance, that some of ancient Israel's most creative theologies were spawned. The realities of Israel's experiences contradicted the promises that the prophets proclaimed. But cognitive dissonance did not produce the complete abandonment of faith. Neither did the theologians merely reiterate what was in the traditions. Rather, the faithful tried to make sense of their faith in the light of their present circumstances. The Bible does not take human experience lightly. Neither should we. Moreover, it is not only the experience of a particular people or a faith-community that matters. To be sure, those are the concerns of most of the Bible. In the wisdom tradition, however, the concern is with the experience of the ordinary human being. Sometimes the realities of life contradict what we have always known to be true and, in the face of that contradiction, we can only admit that we do not understand all of creation.

One learns this from the book of Job. At the outset of the book we are told that Job is righteous; he is a fearer of God. From the standpoint of the orthodox traditions, however, there can be no question as to why he suffers: He must have done something wrong to deserve his pain. So Job's friends come along to confront him, appealing to the standard explanations for human suffering. Eliphaz even reports that he received a supernatural word and visions confirming the orthodox position. He had a divine revelation, he claims (Job 4:12–21). The friends of Job refuse to listen to his testimony and his insistence of innocence. They see no evidence that he had done wrong, but they are certain that there has to be something wrong with him. They know the nature of truth because that is what they have always been taught. They are sure that they know God and God's ways. So they feel right about defending the truth and protecting the integrity of God. For Job's friends, the standard explanations have priority over human testimony. Dogma takes precedence over human pain. The experience of their friend and neighbor Job matters less than the truth they are sure they know. But Job's innocence is a given, according to the prologue. And the epilogue asserts the same, indeed, attributing to God the judgment that Job was right and his friends wrong (Job 42:7). In the end the book does not account for the suffering of the innocent. It implicitly concedes that there is no answer in this case—neither in special revelation, nor in human wisdom. But the book does call into question the easy answers of orthodoxy, even the claim to special revelation. The speeches of God in the book of Job make clear that there are realities about creation that have not been revealed. There are truths that no mortal can grasp, truths that have not been revealed. Whether intentionally or not, the book points to the incompleteness of the creation accounts in Genesis. The world is not as orderly as it seems, and we do not know everything there is to know about creation.

Perhaps even more so than the book of Job, Ecclesiastes conveys wisdom's message that there are some things about creation that will remain a mystery to mortals. For Ecclesiastes, observation of the world reveals not the order and reasonable conduct that one might desire to find, but inconsistencies, contradictions, and inexplicable situations. So Ecclesiastes frequently speaks of what he observes or knows to be true and what he recognizes to be normative, but he quickly points out that there are inconsistencies, even outright contradictions.

For Job and Ecclesiastes, many things about creation remain a mystery. Creation is not as orderly as one would like to believe. To be sure, the wisdom tradition as a whole recognizes that God is the Creator of the universe, but in contrast to the creation accounts in Genesis, wisdom also concedes that God's creation does include many irregularities and unevenness— anomalies that no human being can explain or change. That is the way things are. So one reads in Ecclesiastes:

> What is crooked cannot be made straight,
> What is not there cannot be counted.
> (Eccl. 1:15)

> See the work of God;
> For who can make straight what he has made crooked?
> (Eccl. 7:13–14)

Wisdom's perspective is admittedly heterodox when judged by the viewpoints of the Torah and the Prophets. The entire corpus of wisdom books defies any attempt to systematize the Old Testament in terms of a definite center. There is not one perspective in the Bible, but many. The Bible is heterotextual.

For some scholars, the distinctiveness of wisdom's approach is such that

questions must be raised about its legitimacy and authority. Hence, it is said
that wisdom is of foreign origin and has no authority for people of faith.[19]
Or, as it is more commonly held, wisdom is secular and nontheological. Yet
such an approach misses the theological significance of the tradition. Indeed, one might consider wisdom's contribution to be a corrective to the
dominant voice of the mainstream. Wisdom's "theology from below"
(starting with the plight of humanity) is in fact a necessary counterpoint to
the dominant "theology from above" (starting with "thus saith the LORD").
The wisdom literature is thus a persistent reminder to us that we should not
be too sure that we speak for God and too slow to admit that we stand with
the rest of humanity before the mysteries of God and in the face of life's
contradictions. In the wisdom literature we are instructed not to ignore nature, science, reason, and experience. We are instructed not to ignore the
doubting voices of humanity.

My appeal for a place for reason and experience is, therefore, an appeal
for a more wholesome, yes, a more *canonical* response to the problems that
human beings face. I call for an approach to the issue of homosexuality that
balances the perspectives of Torah and the Prophets with the perspective
of Wisdom. The way of wisdom, which gives credence to science and experience, is not at all unscriptural. It merely assumes a different textual orientation, one that ironically points beyond the written texts.

Some Personal Observations

The sages recognize that neither human observation nor experiences can
be absolutely reliable. There are some risks when one turns to them. Yet it
is necessary for people to live with risks; we have no choice in the matter, for
there are still many things in creation that are not revealed to us. God is in
Wholly Other, but we are mere mortals. We cannot be too sure that we
know the ways of God. We take the risks because we are human. Like the
sages who gave us the wisdom tradition, we live knowing that what we see
and experience often contradicts what we have always thought to be true.

Since the wisdom tradition points us beyond texts to consider observation and experience, I want to conclude by telling of my own experience. I
used to believe that divorce is wrong under any circumstance, simply because that is what the scriptures teach. I could—and still can—quote chapter and verse from the Bible, particularly the words of Jesus. I have since
learned from friends and loved ones what horrible traps bad marriages can
be. People suffer enormously; some people even kill themselves because of
bad marriages that they cannot otherwise escape. Some people suffer physical abuse in such marriages. Some are even killed. Unlike the friends of
Job, I am not willing to uphold dogma at all costs, certainly not when I
know that people are suffering and dying. I have gone back to reread the
scriptures and I have heard the gospel anew.

I also used to believe that homosexual acts are always wrong. Listening to gay and lesbian students and friends, however, I have had to rethink my position and reread the scriptures. Seeing how gay and lesbian people suffer discrimination, face the rejection of family and friends, risk losing their jobs, and live in fear of being humiliated and bashed, I cannot see how anyone would prefer to live that way. I do not understand it all, but I am persuaded that it is not a matter of choice. Seeing how some gay and lesbian couples relate to one another in loving partnerships, observing how much joy they find in one another, and seeing that some of them are better parents than most of us ever will be, I have reconsidered my views. I was wrong.

From the testimony of homosexual persons and from various reports, I have learned that there is an extraordinarily high rate of suicide among homosexual persons. People are dying every day because of society's attitudes—indeed, because of the church's stance. Many people hate themselves because of what society and the church say about them. I know of many homosexual persons in the ministry who have been very effective for the cause of Jesus Christ, but they suffer tremendous guilt because they have to keep their secret from the church they love dearly. I have met many students here at the Princeton Seminary who have a strong sense of the call to ministry and all the obvious gifts for it, but they cannot obey their call because of who they are. They are hurt by the church. I cannot believe that we are called to perpetuate such pain and suffering in the world. I am compelled now to trust my observations and experience.

For me there is nothing less than the gospel at stake. I have no choice but to take the testimonies of gays and lesbians seriously. I do so with some comfort, however, for the scriptures themselves give me the warrant to trust that human beings can know truths apart from divine revelation.

NOTES

1. The text says nothing of homoerotic acts between women. Indeed, in all the Bible there is only one reference to female-female sexual acts: Rom. 1:26. This is a significant fact, for it may cast some light on biblical perspectives on the function of sex. Male-male sexual intercourse was abhorrent because the "seed," which is meant for human reproduction, is wasted. For the same reason, Onan's spilling of his "seed" on the ground was condemned. He was supposed to give an offspring to his deceased brother by having sexual intercourse with his sister-in-law (although he was not required to marry her), but he spilled his "seed" (Gen. 38:1–11). Thus, *coitus interruptus* (the withdrawal method of birth control) was considered abhorrent. Later traditions even considered male masturbation wrong, hence the term "onanism." As for the reference in Rom. 1:26, it is important to observe that the language of "exchange" may suggest that idolatry is at issue. In v. 23, Paul says "they *exchanged* the glory of the immortal God for images," (italics mine) and in

v. 25 he says "they exchanged the truth about God for a lie and worshiped and served the creature rather than the Creator." The language echoes what one finds in Hos. 4:7, "they changed their glory for shame." The issue there is Israel's idolatry; the Israelites of the Northern Kingdom exchanged the Glory-presence of God for an idol and followed the ways of the Canaanites (compare Hos. 10:5).

2. See also Ex. 21:17. The Hebrew verb *qillēl* does not just mean "to curse" (so NRSV; NIV), but literally "to make light, to slight." See Lev. 19:4; Judg. 9:27; 2 Sam. 16:5, 7, 10, 11, 13. Thus, NJPS translates the verb as "insult," while NEB has "revile." The Aphel of the verb in Aramaic means "to dishonor, disrespect." The Akkadian cognate is *qullulu*, "to reduce, diminish, discredit." The Hebrew verb is, thus, the opposite of *kibbēd*, "to honor" (literally, "make important, heavy").

3. See Simon B. Parker, "The Hebrew Bible and Homosexuality," *Quarterly Review* 11, no. 3 (1991): 5–8.

4. See my discussion of this passage in "Textual Orientation," *Biblical Ethics and Homosexuality: Listening to Scripture*, ed. Robert Brawley (Louisville, Ky.: Westminster John Knox Press, 1996).

5. See "A Princeton Declaration: Upholding the PC(USA) in the Decision Not to Ordain Individuals Engaged in Homosexual Practice," Spring 1993.

6. See the contribution of Richard E. Whitaker in this volume.

7. James B. Pritchard, ed., *Ancient Near Eastern Texts Relating to the Old Testament*, 3d ed. with supplements (Princeton: Princeton University Press, 1969), 60–72.

8. According to the Atraḥasis Epic, humanity had increased and become too noisy for the gods, and hence the gods' desire for limitations. See Anne Kilmer, "The Mesopotamian Concept of Overpopulation and Its Solution as Represented in Mythology," *Orientalia* 41 (1972):160–77 and William J. Moran, "The Babylonian Story of the Flood," *Biblica* 40 (1971):51–61.

9. See Tikva Frymer-Kensky, "The Atraḥasis Epic and Its Significance for Our Understanding of Genesis 1–9," *Biblical Archaeologist* 40 (1977):150.

10. Gerhard von Rad, *Old Testament Theology* I, trans. D.M.G. Stalker (New York: Harper & Row, 1962), 418.

11. See Klaus Koch, "Is There a Doctrine of Retribution in the Old Testament?" in *Theodicy in the Old Testament* (Issues in Religion and Theology 4), ed. J. L. Crenshaw (Philadelphia/London: Fortress/SPCK, 1983), 57–87.

12. See Ronald E. Clements, *Wisdom in Theology* (Grand Rapids/Exeter: Eerdmans/Paternoster, 1992), 65–93.

13. See John J. Collins, "The Biblical Precedent for Natural Theology," *Journal of the American Academy of Religion* 41, no. 5, Supplement (March 1977): 35–67.

14. See "Wisdom and Pastoral Theology," *Andover-Newton Quarterly* 7, no. 1 (1966):10.

15. Glendon Bryce, " 'Better'-Proverbs: An Historical and Structural Study," in *The Society of Biblical Literature One Hundred Eighth Annual Meeting: Book of Seminar Papers* II, ed. L. C. McGaughy (Missoula, Mont.: SBL, 1972), 343–54.

16. See W. Brueggemann, *In Man We Trust: The Neglected Side of Biblical Faith* (Atlanta: John Knox Press, 1972).
17. "The Renewed Authority of Old Testament Wisdom for Contemporary Faith," in *Canon and Authority: Essays in Old Testament Religion and Theology*, ed. G. W. Coats and B. O. Long (Philadelphia: Fortress Press, 1977), 146.
18. Indeed, James Barr has recently argued in *Biblical Faith and Natural Theology* (Oxford: Clarendon Press, 1993, 195) that "natural theology" is not found only in wisdom literature; it is in fact a biblical viewpoint, evident in both the Old Testament and the New. So Barr concludes: "If the presence of natural theology within the Bible is recognized, it may mean that common ideas of the doctrine of scripture have to be revised."
19. So, for instance, Hartmut Gese, *Lehre und Wirklichkeit in der alten Weisheit* (Tübingen: Mohr, 1958), 3; Horst D. Preuss, *Der Segen in der Bibel und im Handeln der Kirche* (Munich: Kaiser, 1968), 40–42.

3
Reading and Understanding the
New Testament on Homosexuality

Brian K. Blount

In his article "Relations Natural and Unnatural," Richard B. Hays concludes that even after we have determined what Paul believed regarding homosexuality, we must still determine "how to construe the authority of his opinion in the present time."[1] He writes,

> Because there remain open questions about precisely *how* the Bible functions as an authority for normative ethical judgments, we cannot relieve ourselves of the responsibility for moral decision by appealing to the plain sense of single prooftext; nor, on the other hand should we feel constrained to force Paul, through exegetical contortions, to say what we think he ought to have said. We must let the text have its say, whether for us or against us; then we must decide what obedience to God requires. . . . The debate turns on questions concerning the *appropriation* of the biblical teachings in later historical settings.[2]

There is no question that the New Testament rarely speaks about homosexual activity; but when it does (in 1 Cor. 6:9, Rom. 1:24–28, and 1 Tim. 1:10), it does so negatively. The conclusion is sure: "Paul does not believe that homosexuality is an acceptable way of living."[3] As Hays warns, appeals to "exegetical contortions" will, in the end, fail to convince the careful reader that Paul was anything less than emphatically negative on the subject. The apostle presents his concern in the form of an ethical prescription condemning the practice for those who would call themselves Christian. It is no wonder, then, that many Christians agree with the sentiment expressed in the editorial section of the Dallas *Times Herald* on March 31, 1978.

> I can much more easily respect and understand an atheist or agnostic accepting homosexuality than an individual who alleges to take the Bible seriously. Scripture is unequivocal on the subject,

and to interpret it in any other way is to play fast and loose with God's word.[4]

The situation is not, however, as indisputable as the author of the editorial protests. Simply knowing what the scriptures say, in this case what Paul said about homosexual activity for his time, does not determine how we are to interpret those Pauline texts for our time. At the interpretative level, which is as important as the exegetical one, other considerations can and must be made. Reading is not always understanding. No doubt this was what Hays meant when he suggested that "we cannot relieve ourselves of the responsibility for moral decision by appealing to the plain sense of a single prooftext. . . ." Though we might increase the number from one to three proof texts, the argument is the same. It is also incumbent upon us to *understand* what Paul said, why he said it in his own time and place, and whether and how it applies to contemporary Christians in the time and place that make up the latter days of the twentieth century. The task of the contemporary Christian goes beyond the mere formality of reading the text by surveying and deciphering the words across its pages. Understanding necessitates an appropriation of the text for Christian living in the contemporary circumstance.

Textual understanding requires a great deal more patience and study than a mere reading of the text. Although the processes of reading and understanding may produce the same conclusions about its meaning, very often they will not. Indeed, this is precisely the situation we find when we interpret Paul's statements on homosexual activity. Every literate person who picks up the texts can read them, but not everyone will take the time and effort to understand them. Our task in this chapter is to push beyond the elementary level of reading the prooftexts on the surface. Our goal is to understand Paul's message, particularly that part of the message that has imperative application for our own time.

I want to begin by explaining, very simplistically, my method of understanding biblical texts. I believe that God works through human beings and has inspired the human authors of these texts to write as they have written. God's message becomes the central indicative faith statement, which, in turn, becomes the foundation for their message. Yet because God inspires and does not overwhelm human messengers, they are not mere tape recorders who transcribe God's word in a vacuum. Instead they interpret that word through their own historical circumstance and the presuppositions of that circumstance. Already, then, the faith statement they present is an *interpretation,* an *understanding* of what God has given them. They are not merely repeating the dictation of God's words; they are interpreting God's Word. Later, when these authors give imperative direction for ethical behavior based on their faith statements, they are making even more of an interpretive move; they are adapting their indicative message to concrete situations in the life of a specific human community.

When I approach the text, I ask, therefore, What is the indicative foundation that directs the ethical prescriptions? How has the human circumstance influenced not only the imperative prescriptions, but also the indicative faith understanding that drives them? Is there a way to take the basic inspired message and apply it to our new social-historical circumstance? Most importantly, are there changes in our social-historical circumstance that mandate a reevaluation of the imperative prescriptions of the biblical authors? Is it possible that we may be able—and even required, given our new context—to bring the indicative faith statement in the apostolic writings to imperative life in a way that is distinct from the way the apostolic writers themselves brought it to imperative life in their time and circumstance?

In other words, we want to consider whether Paul's discussion on the particular issue of homosexual activity was influenced more by his social and historical circumstance than by his indicative faith pronouncement. If this is so, we may not only recognize that Paul is reflecting the contemporary ethical prescriptions of his time rather than transcending them. We may also consider whether we might, today, make different ethical prescriptions that would more faithfully reflect Paul's indicative principle than Paul's own ethical pronouncements did.

Before going forward, we should note a possible objection. One might well argue that there is no precedent for reevaluating an ethical position as it is stated in a New Testament text because that position is determined more by the influence of the author's social context than by his indicative faith foundation. I would disagree. The precedent is Paul himself.

For example, on the imperative statements about divorce the writers of the synoptic gospels (Matthew, Mark, Luke) are clear. Jesus' mediation of the scriptural rule on divorce prompts him to speak against it (Mark 10:2–9). He may allow it in Matthew for sexual misconduct (Matt. 5:31–32; 19:1–12), but, apparently, this is the only viable reason for divorce. In 1 Cor. 7:10–16, Paul agrees with this imperative reality when giving ethical advice on the matter. In verses 10–11, he clearly states, *in the voice of the Lord*, that divorce and remarriage are unacceptable. Yet in verses 12–16, this time under his own apostolic authority, *not that of the Lord*, he modifies Jesus' recorded teaching precisely because of a shift in context. Evidently, he did not think that Jesus' divorce imperative was integrally tied into Jesus' faith pronouncement about the coming of God's rule. Thus, whereas the tradition shows Jesus prohibiting divorce, Paul boldly adds a marital "escape clause" that would allow a new Christian to divorce a pagan spouse who disapproved of the conversion. Since Jesus' earthly mission was directed only at the Jews, it is no wonder that the traditions about his ministry divulge no such concern for the problems this kind of mixed marriage could create. Paul believed that it was more important that a Christian remain a Christian than return to paganism to appease a disgruntled partner. Hence he offered a change of Jesus' ethical position that was more in harmony with Jesus' mediation of God's authority than Jesus' own position was, given the historical changes that had occurred since Jesus' ministry. I am suggesting that as the Spirit guided Paul to understand the Jesus tradition in this manner, so, too, the Spirit can guide Christians today.

Paul's Variety of Perspectives

I want to offer the hypothesis, with Richard Longenecker in his book *New Testament Social Ethics for Today*, that Paul's indicative foundation is his eschatological (that is, ultimate) understanding of what God is doing redemptively through Jesus Christ.[5] When Paul operates directly from this indicative foundation in making imperative-ethical statements, he tends to emphasize images of equality, freedom, and radical inclusion. Galatians 3:28 is a prime example. When, however, Paul operates from a foundation of thought that is more directly linked to his Hellenistic Jewish background, he is preoccupied less with what God is doing presently and will do momentarily through Christ, and more with what God did do in creation according to the Hebrew scriptures. When Paul operates from this foundation of creation, he tends to stress images of order and natural appropriateness that are very much akin to the manner in which those images are ethically expressed in his culture, specifically the Hellenistic Jewish culture of his historical context. When he argues from his understanding of creation, he mirrors rather than transcends the patriarchal cultural norms of his time. When he argues directly from his eschatological (ultimate) and redemptive understanding, he tends to push beyond their limiting, normative boundaries.

Longenecker uses Paul's treatment of women as his primary case in point. Paul's statements regarding women demand an attentive process of understanding. At times statements in the apostle's ethical writings appear to demand a secondary status for women, whereas at other times he appears to prescribe a gender equity of responsibility to God and others. Indeed, sometimes the apostle appears to present both positions within the space of a single discussion.

Paul in 1 Corinthians

In 1 Corinthians 7, Paul appears to be operating from the faith understanding of God's redemptive actions in Jesus Christ and how humans are to respond to those actions. Males and females in marital relationships have, as they do in Gal. 3:28, an equal sense of responsibility and freedom before God. "It would have been easy for Paul, in keeping with the times, to have reserved all of the rights for men and to have laid all of the responsibilities on women. In 1 Corinthians 7, however, Paul speaks of men and women in the family as being accountable to one another in commensurate ways, with both possessing rights and obligations."[6]

However, in 1 Cor. 11:2–16, a text that discusses whether and how women are to speak and act in worship, Paul's theological understanding of God's redemptive work through Christ is mixed with his emphasis on creation. The result is the intermixing of traditional and progressive attitudes about women in worship. Finally, in 1 Cor. 14:34–35 (which many scholars perceive to be so thoroughly conservative and simplistic in its insistence on the subordination of women that it must be a secondary insertion into the Pauline text), the argument from creation leads to a specific ordering of human relations that clearly subordinates women.

Longenecker recognizes the influence that context has upon the apostle's ethical decision making: "When circumstances within the churches urged on him a more moderate course, he seems at times to have argued more from the categories of creation and curse than from the categories of eschatological redemption in Christ. At such times he appears, when judged from our present perspective, almost chauvinistic."[7] Indeed, as Victor Furnish demonstrates in his book *The Moral Teaching of Paul*, it seems clear that Paul's conservatism with regard to women in worship has very little to do with his understanding of God's redemptive activity, and everything to do with his cultural bias. When the apostle demands that a woman's decorum in worship honor both God and her husband, and that, therefore, she should have a sign of authority covering her head, he is drawing from the ordering concept of creation, which very much follows the interpretative line taken in the rest of Jewish society at the time.

> One must realize that Paul has no special crochet about women veiling their heads. It is something he believes ought to be taken for granted. It is not his innovation but a part of his culture. In Judaism it was strictly forbidden that a woman should be seen in public with an uncovered head. . . . In non-Jewish circles as well it was commonly believed to be immodest for a woman to go about bareheaded.[8]

However, when operating from the perspective of redemption, as he does exclusively in 1 Corinthians 7 and intermittently in 1 Cor. 11:2–16, he asserts female equality. "What Paul appears to be saying, in effect, is that though he has argued on the basis of creation for the subordination of women in worship, on the basis of redemption he must also assert their equality."[9]

Longenecker's hypothesis is also applicable to Paul's statements on homosexual activity. I would offer that when Paul makes these statements, as when he makes his statements about the subordinate status of women, he is operating directly from his understanding of the creation concept. Homosexual acts are therefore unnatural in the sense that they do not meet the sexual order described in the Genesis accounts of procreation.[10] They are acts that result from idolatry. Because of humankind's idolatrous rebellion against God, God gives humankind up to its own devices. The lust that produces homosexual activity is just one of the results of this idolatrous behavior.

Paul's assessment agrees with the philosophical and religious norms of the time. Secular philosophers in Paul's time considered homosexual activity a negative behavior, "especially when they compare[d] it with a heterosexual relationship or marriage."[11] For Seneca, a distinguished tutor and adviser to the Emperor Nero, homosexual activity was looked upon as one of the grosser forms of self-indulgence; it was driven by lust. In Plutarch, another secular contemporary of Paul's, it was love between a man and woman that was recognized as natural. The problem with homosexual activity was that it was unnatural and, therefore, dehumanizing. As Victor Furnish writes: "In Plutarch's dialogue there is a concern for the sexual exploitation that homosexuality involves, even where there is consent. There is also the typically Stoic aversion to whatever is 'contrary to nature.' "[12] Dio Chrysostom, another secular contemporary, also saw homosexual activity as exploitive. Like Seneca, he recognized lust as the root of the problem. Hellenistic Jews like Philo of Alexandria held a similar view. As Furnish notes, for them "[s]uch behavior is said to contravene 'the law of nature' and to spring from unbridled lust."[13] We will see that Paul had exactly the same two primary concerns.

We therefore need to direct our attention specifically at the key texts. The first is 1 Cor. 6:9. Chronologically, this is Paul's first statement on this issue, and it is also his least understandable. Here Paul uses two words that are today taken to refer to male homosexual activity; such people will not inherit the kingdom of God, according to Paul. The two key words in this vice list are *malakoi* and *arsenokoitai*, Greek terms that really have no adequate English translation. Since the root of the first word means soft or weak, and thus effeminate, it is usually assumed to refer to the more passive homosexual partner. The second term, compounded from the roots for "male" and "cohabit," most likely means the more active homosexual partner.

What we do know from the context is that Paul is discussing sexual immorality (1 Corinthians 5—6). He is responding to an oral report about a man who is cohabiting with his stepmother (5:1). Whereas it appears the Corinthians themselves did not seem too bothered by the situation, Paul demands quick corrective action. In 6:1–11, he talks about the impropriety of Christians taking disputes to secular courts and, in the midst of this discussion, he speaks of those who are in the world (the judges of the secular courts) and those who are not (the Christians.) In order to make his point concrete, he spells out the kinds of people who are of the world (like the judges), people who behave the way the Corinthians evidently once did. To do this he uses a vice list that in verse 9 includes the two key terms, *malakoi* and *arsenokoitai*. No doubt, in using these words Paul is thinking of the Gentile background of some of the Christians in Corinth, as 6:11 makes clear. What is interesting is that in this verse, which is so ethically charged, "[t]he words Paul uses in the catalogue for homosexual behavior (assuming he *is* using them with that reference) suggests that the picture in his mind is approximately that which one gets of the practice from the contemporary authors cited above."[14] Driven by lust, the one partner has violated the male role that is by nature his, and by taking advantage of this, the other person has also violated his male role.[15]

Paul in Romans

Romans 1:26–28 is the other key text. Here the text is more specific about describing homosexual activity and, for the first and only time in the Bible, female homosexual activity is condemned. Once again, we note that the literary context is one that cites the influence of Gentile immorality. Furnish notes that after a careful evaluation of the text, one is struck by the similarities between Paul's condemnation of homosexual behavior and that of his non-Christian contemporaries. Both Paul and his contemporaries see homosexual behavior as something freely chosen by an individual. They all associate homosexual behavior with insatiable lust; Paul uses language filled with passion. And they all regard such behavior as a violation of the created order. So Furnish concludes: "These similarities make it reasonable to suppose that the picture of homosexual practices Paul had in his mind correspond closely to the depiction of it we have seen in the works of Seneca, Dio Chrysostom, and Philo."[16]

Indeed, when one compares the writings of Paul's contemporaries—Seneca, Plutarch, Dio Chrysostom, the Hellenistic Jew Philo, the Hellenistic Jewish writing Wisdom of Solomon, or general Stoic philosophy—one finds that they all have very similar condemnation of homosexual behavior, and they all associate homosexual activity with idolatry, lust, and a disregard for the natural order. Paul's attitude on homosexuality was no different than that of his contemporaries.

In Romans, Paul explains that the world itself is a testimony to God's sovereignty, and thus the Gentiles have knowledge of God (even apart from the Law) and have no excuse for failing to recognize God as Lord. The worst thing is that they worship and serve not the Creator, but the creature. Their problem was idolatry. This is the fundamental way in which humans fail to recognize the Lordship of God. Thus, because of this key sin of idolatry, God gives the Gentiles up to their impurity. In an argument that is very similar to what we find in Hellenistic Judaism, particularly in the Wisdom of Solomon, Paul warns that their wickedness will generate its own punishment. God gives the Gentiles up to the consequences of their idolatry. Here, once again, we see how Paul's ethical imperative is heavily influenced by his moral-social context. As Victor Furnish argues, "In these closing paragraphs Paul is also being influenced by the traditional connection made in Hellenistic Judaism between idolatry and sexual immorality."[17] It is indeed, then, not surprising to find that one of the primary punishments that Paul envisions for idolatry is the evil of homosexual behavior, what he sees as a sexual immorality that is lust driven and unnatural.

Paul is operating here from his understanding of creation; male and female are to be joined sexually for procreative purposes only. Therefore, he stresses "natural" appropriateness, and calls for judgment against those who move away from God's intended desires for creation—as Genesis describes it. When the indicative foundation that is consistently central to Paul's message throughout his writings surfaces in this context in Romans, however, it is not the foundation for a continuation of this kind of warning. Rather, it is the insistence that the grace of God through Jesus Christ offers mercy to both the pagan Gentiles who commit such sins of idolatry and the Jews who think they are better than the Gentiles because of the law (Rom. 3:21–26).[18] Where Paul's discussion based on creation has defined how and why persons are *excluded* on the basis of their rebellion against God and the created order God has established, the move towards what God has done, is doing, and will do in Christ Jesus offers an opportunity of *inclusion* for all.

Conclusion

What this historical and literary-theological review demonstrates is that Paul's undeniably negative view of homosexual behavior is not derived so much from his indicative pronouncement of God's gift of the Christ as it is a reflection of the moral climate of his own time. In fact, as Furnish observes, Paul "assumes that homosexual conduct is symptomatic of an individual's fundamental refusal to acknowledge God."[19] To be sure, most contemporary scholars do not hold that the root cause of homosexual activity is idolatry. The connection between homosexuality and idolatry, taken for granted in Paul's religious and secular environment, is not assumed in modern society. For Paul, since homosexual activity was inextricably tied up with idolatry, there was absolutely no way that a person could engage in homosexual acts and at the same time be "in Christ." If we no longer perceive that homosexuality is the result of idolatry, however, we may consider the possibility that a person may be at once homosexual and in Christ. Hence, if one could today acknowledge what Paul would never have considered (that a homosexual person need not necessarily be an idolater and that he or she can acknowledge the indicative of God's revelation in Christ), Paul's primary complaint may well be taken away.

What is certain is that this issue is not a significant part of Paul's indicative program. Furnish points to an anecdote that details the plight of a local television host who was to have a gay-rights leader on his show. The television personality called Furnish because he wanted to confront the gay rights leader with biblical injunctions against homosexual activity, but did not know where to look. Furnish observes: "That interviewer had already discovered something important, although he scarcely realized it: *homosexuality is not a prominent biblical concern.*"[20] That we are not dealing with a fundamental biblical theme is brought to light by the reality that we have to hunt for relevant passages on the issue. It is not a fundamental part of the indicative principle of Paul's faith. I would argue, therefore, that his ethic on this issue, clear though it may be, is more an imperative application of his social reality than it is an imperative application of his indicative faith reality.

Furthermore, I would argue for a reevaluation of our position regarding contemporary homosexuality. Our context forces a shift in the way we understand homosexuality, as opposed to the way Paul and his followers understood it. Chief among these differences is the concept of what is natural. Liberationist interpreters argue that "natural" is often used as a code word for what a predominant group considers socially acceptable and is, therefore, always to be viewed skeptically. We should also recognize that in our twentieth-century context, sexuality is no longer viewed as natural simply and only because of its connection with procreation, as Paul and his contemporaries did. There is a sense of intimacy and pleasure connected with sexuality, particularly in monogamous, responsible, enduring relationships that need not include procreation for the relationship to be considered natural. For the ancients, Paul included, homosexuality was a negative *act* because it was contrary to the "natural" procreative ordering of male and female. We now believe that there is much more than mere action involved. We believe that lifestyle and identity are defining human realities that have priority over any actual act. We are thus called to reevaluate the understanding of homosexual relationships as relationships, something the ancients neither considered nor even conceived. They may well be as natural as any other in our modern context—if intimacy, reciprocity and responsibility are the markers of human relationship rather than procreation.

The contextual reality that drove Paul and his contemporaries, both Greek and Jewish, to condemn homosexual activity has shifted dramatically. It can no longer be understood to have the same causes and connections assumed in the ancient world. This does not mean that we then automatically shift our interpretative position. But it does call us to question whether Paul's statement derives from his indicative reality about what God is doing in the world through Jesus Christ or whether it represents his contextual understanding of that message in the light of his Jewish background, most notably his sense of creation and the natural order. If it does connect more to his own contextual situation, then we are prompted to push beyond his imperative, ethical observations, and make our own ethical decisions. We do so not according to Paul's contextuality, but according to his indicative reality. That indicative reality remains our own, and in its interaction with our socio-historical context, it provides the basis for our ethical decisions. We are, therefore, called not simply to read Paul into the twentieth century, but to understand him for, and in light of, the twentieth-century context. And if his own writings are to be any guide, when Paul draws ethical direction for his churches from his understanding of what God is doing ultimately through Jesus Christ, he does so in a way that brings radical newness and inclusion.

NOTES

1. Richard B. Hays, "Relations Natural and Unnatural: A Response to J. Boswell's Exegesis of Romans 1," *Journal of Religious Ethics* 14, no. 1 (1986):205.
2. Ibid.
3. Robert F. O'Toole, *Who Is a Christian?: A Study in Pauline Ethics* (Collegeville, Minn.: Liturgical Press, 1990), 116.
4. Quoted in Victor P. Furnish, *The Moral Teaching of Paul* (Nashville: Abingdon Press, 1979), 52.
5. Richard Longenecker, *New Testament Social Ethics for Today* (Grand Rapids: Wm. B. Eerdmans Publishing Co., 1984). The extensive debate that centers around Paul's indicative "core" or "coherent center" of thought, whether such a core exists, or even if one should pursue an identification of it has produced much more material than can be considered in a single chapter. Logistical concerns demand that we define the terminology only as much as is necessary for the purposes of our study. I have therefore presented this rather general offering as the foundation for Paul's thought. Researchers agree, however, that any attempt to locate a coherent center to Paul's thought is a precarious one. Paul was not a systematic theologian. The very form of his communication (letter) indicates a desire to write words "on target" to specific communities. Still, as Jouette Bassler notes, despite the fact that Paul was no systematic theologian, there does seem ". . . to be a pattern, a center, a communication, a set of beliefs, a narrative, a coherence—something—in Paul's thoughts or behind them that dispels any abiding sense of mere opportunism or intellectual chaos on the part of the apostle." See Jouette M. Bassler, "Paul's Theology: Whence and Whither?," *Pauline Theology: Volume II, 1 & 2 Corinthians*, ed. David Hay (Minneapolis: Fortress Press, 1993), 6. This central vision, this indicative foundation, was always applied in a highly contingent manner.
6. Ibid., 78.
7. Ibid., 87.

8. Furnish, 96–97.
9. Longenecker, 80–81.
10. Hays, on page 191, notes that "The reference to God as creator would certainly evoke for Paul, as well as for his readers, immediate recollections of the creation story in Genesis 1—3."
11. Furnish, 60.
12. Ibid., 62.
13. Ibid., 65.
14. Ibid., 72.
15. Ibid.
16. Ibid., 73.
17. Ibid., 77.
18. Note Hays and others who argue that 1:26–27 must be kept in contact with chapter 2. This argument that includes Jew and Gentile moves to the grace discussion of chapter 3.
19. Furnish, 79.
20. Ibid., 53.

4

Creation, Sexuality, and Homosexuality in the New Testament

Ulrich W. Mauser

The issue of homosexuality in society and in the church has become one of the most passionately discussed issues in recent years. Within that discussion, biblical statements about homosexuality have received intense study and produced widely divergent interpretations. In most of those studies of biblical texts, the problem of homosexuality is isolated from the broader question about the positive ethos of human sexuality in the Bible. I consider this isolation a serious mistake. This chapter seeks to place the most important passage on homosexuality in the New Testament, in Rom. 1:18–32, in the context of other New Testament discussions in which the sexual ethos of the Christian community is clarified by reference to the creation stories in Genesis 1—2.

In several New Testament passages dealing with aspects of the relationship between men and women, we find an appeal to the Old Testament creation stories in Genesis 1—2. These passages are fundamental for New Testament perceptions of human sexuality. The passages are (1) Mark 10:2–9 and its parallel, Matt. 19:3–9, (2) Rom. 1:18–32, specifically vv. 24–27, (3) 1 Cor. 6:12–20, (4) 1 Cor. 11:2–16, and (5) Eph. 5:21–33. We shall consider Rom. 1:18–32 last because it is the passage that most explicitly deals with homosexuality. Consideration of Eph. 5:21–33 will be omitted because space does not permit its inclusion.

Addressing Sexual Behavior

The New Testament passages mentioned above have in common an appeal to the Genesis story of creation for the purpose of giving guidance about sexual attitudes and conduct. We shall now proceed to look more closely at the linkage between the creation stories and the specific issues raised in each of the four passages under consideration. The dominant question will be throughout: What are the reasons, the purpose, and the result of the authors' practice to address questions of sexual behavior in the earliest Christian communities by connecting them with the creation stories of Genesis 1—2?

Divorce: Mark 10:2–9 and Matt. 19:3–9

In these similar passages Pharisees challenge Jesus with the question of whether it is lawful to end a marriage by divorce. Although the two accounts show considerable differences, the appeal to Gen. 1:27 and 2:24 in relation to divorce is almost the same. Jesus' answer to his questioners goes behind Mosaic legislation, back to the creation stories. He says (following Mark 10:6–8): "from the beginning of creation, 'God made them male and female' (Gen. 1:27). 'For this reason a man shall leave his father and mother and be joined to his wife, and the two shall become one flesh' " (Gen. 2:24). What is expressed in the appeal to creation?

The Mosaic law permitting and regulating divorce is superseded by an older, more original, order of sexuality. The appeal reaches back to an order of things that prevailed "at, or from, the beginning" (Matt. 19:4; Mark 10:6). Moses' law opens the door to a possibility that, at the beginning in God's creation, was not given. The appeal to creation against Moses' Torah presupposes the restoration of a state of human sexuality in which adjustments to sick and destroyed relationships between husbands and wives are no longer necessary. The idea of the correspondence of primal time and final time is introduced into the concept of human sexuality: With the coming of the kingdom of God a restored condition of the husband-wife relation has arrived that confirms God's good, pristine order.

Genesis 1 and 2 were, in New Testament times, read as a single continuous narrative. Thus the statement about the creation of male and female (Gen. 1:27) and the sentence about the leaving of the parental home by the husband to cling to his wife, forming a new oneness out of two (Gen. 2:24), are welded into a single statement in which the former sentence becomes the reason for the second: "God made them male and female. *For this reason* a man shall leave his father and mother and be joined to his wife, and the two shall become one flesh" (Mark 10:6–8; Matt. 19:4–5 with negligible differences; italics mine). The drive that causes a man to abandon his family's unit to form with his wife a new union of life is grounded in an antecedent act of divine creation, the calling into being of the single human species in the two different forms of male and female (Gen. 1:27). As God's creation, there is only one human being who exists in two separate, distinct, and different forms of male and female. On the other side of the same coin, they are in their separateness, distinction, and difference one single human being. In this simultaneous oneness and duality, male and female together are the image of God, receive the blessing of God and the unrestricted approval of their Creator to be "very good" (Gen. 1:28, 31).

The drift of the debate about divorce in Mark 10 and Matthew 19 leads to ethical conclusions and to moral imperatives: "What God has joined together, let no one separate" (Mark 10:9; Matt. 19:6). But the imperatives are, through their connection with the creation stories, laid on the foundation of a primal facticity that is not subject to, or dependent on, human decision and conduct. Jesus' judgment against divorce is not pegged to a superior morality, but to the divine verdict of creation. Perhaps it is necessary to use philosophical terminology to establish the point most clearly: The words of the creation stories uncover a level of existence prior to morality and law, they are ontologically oriented, not morally directed. The prohibition of divorce is interpreted in Mark 10, and with less force in Matthew 19, as the rediscovery of a state of creation that is foundational for all law and custom.

The truth or falsehood of this vision of the nature of the male-female relationship does not depend on the human ability, or inability, to live up to its demands. The Matthean version of the debate on divorce is, significantly enough, followed up by the disillusioned statement of the disciples: "If such is the case of a man with his wife, it is better not to marry" (Matt. 19:10). Jesus' words were, then, experienced as a provocation, an unwelcome revelation, a jolting out of natural complacency. The condition of our moral sensibilities, and the range of what our self-experiences dictate as achievable, are not the measure with which human sexuality is discovered as God's creation.

Prostitution: 1 Cor. 6:12–20

Here, Paul fights against the view that the affirmation "all things are lawful for me" (6:12) be misused as permission for members of the Christian community in Corinth to hire the services of prostitutes. Manifestly, there was a group among the Corinthian Christians who advocated this practice, and their support of it seems to have appealed to the notion of Christian freedom. They must have reasoned that sexual activity is a purely biological function comparable to the need for food and drink (6:13). As the stomach requires periodic intake of nourishment causing a constant cycle of hunger, satisfaction, and renewed hunger, so sexual activity is governed by the similar cycle of desire, satisfaction, and newly awakened desire. Paul's turn against the apologetic for prostitution is clear: "Shun prostitution" (6:18). Prostitution is not an exercise of Christian freedom, but a form of enslavement both for the prostitute and for the male perpetrator (6:12).

Woven into the argument against prostitution is a direct citation of a part of Gen. 2:24 and a play with words used in the same verse. A male using a prostitute "clings" to her (6:16) as a believer "clings" to the Lord (6:17). The Greek word employed in both verses, *kollōmai*, "to cling," is the

same as the one used in the septuagint version of Gen. 2:24 for the union
of man and woman. A part of Gen. 2:24 is quoted verbatim in 1 Cor. 6:16
"the two shall be one flesh." The Genesis word is pivotal in the context because it states an act in which two persons distinct from each other become
a unity of life. There is, in this respect, an exact parallel between the unity
established by a man and a prostitute and the unity achieved between the
believer and the Lord: "whoever clings to a prostitute becomes one body
with her" and "anyone who clings to the Lord becomes one spirit with him"
(6:16–17).

In distinction to the fuller quotation of Gen. 2:24 in Matt. 19:5 and Mark
10:7–8, Paul concentrates the Genesis word completely into the event in
which two become one; the leaving of the parental home is omitted and the
union of husband and wife is reduced to a mere echo of the word *kollōmai*.
In this way the whole question is reduced to the single point of two becoming one. This becoming one out of two gives rise to the devastating
analogy between the act of prostitution and the act of Christian faith. In the
sentence from the creation story "the two shall be one flesh" Paul heard the
affirmation that the sexual union between a man and a woman establishes
intrinsically a union in which their selves, their personhoods, come together such that each belongs to the other. *Flesh* is not distinct from *body* in
this case as is shown by the parallel between becoming "one body" with the
prostitute, and becoming "one flesh" of husband and wife in 1 Cor. 6:16.
The sexual act involves the body, and not merely the stomach. *Body* de-
notes, as it frequently does with Paul, the total self that, in its corporeality,
is in dependency and communion with the other. The union of two selves
in the sexual act can be in harmony with the union of the believer and the
Lord. But it becomes, in Paul's reading of Gen. 2:24, a contradiction in
terms if it involves intercourse with a prostitute. "Christ is the faithfulness
of God in person, whereas the harlot personifies human unfaithfulness toward other humans" (K. Barth, *Church Dogmatics* III/2, 307, corrected
translation). Union with the prostitute is, therefore, not an expression of
Christian freedom. Rather, it is the destruction of freedom, its perversion
into slavery.

By establishing the analogy between the Christians' unity in the Lord
and the unity of two human selves in the sexual act, Paul also imputed a
meaning to Gen. 2:24 that this verse had never before achieved. Prostitution was not outlawed in the Mosaic Torah. No Jewish interpreter has ever,
to my knowledge, drawn consequences from this sentence in the biblical
creation story leading to the verdict that prostitution was intrinsically and
essentially a contradiction to being a member of the community of God.
The intensity of Paul's understanding of belonging to Christ, of sharing a
new life with him beyond the destructive realities of sin and death, seems
to have intensified also his sensibilities for the dimensions of sexuality. He

incorporated the creation story at the very core of his stand against prostitution, but he also read the Genesis narrative as one who had passed from death to life in his becoming one with Christ. Creation, including human sexuality, remains for him a key for understanding the new creation. But the reverse is also true: It is the "belonging to Christ" that unlocks depths in the understanding of sexuality unfathomed before.

Gender Relations: 1 Cor. 11:2–16

References to Genesis 1—2 are integrated into the entire argument of this passage. The quotes and allusions to the first two chapters in Genesis are applied to a specific problem in the Christian community at Corinth whose precise reconstruction causes extreme difficulties.

It is our assumption that the tension to which Paul addresses himself in this passage arises in the public worship of the community. In view is not a dress code for private gatherings, or for the streets of Corinth, but a regulation dictating proper headdress and hairstyle when the community meets for worship. In this act of worship, women pray aloud and prophesy along with the men, and no criticism of this custom is implied (vv. 4–5). What is controversial, however, is the way some women cut their hair and discard certain pieces of clothing covering their head during public worship (vv. 5–6, 13–15). Men's hairstyles are mentioned, but only by way of contrast (v. 4). The women's appearance is given far more space; it is their problem that sets Paul off on a long and involved discourse.

For our interpretation of the passage we assume that a group of enthusiasts in Corinth interpreted Paul's own teaching as the arrival of a freedom in which material limitations of human life were eliminated. Marriage was to be shunned because it necessitated a bondage to physical realities that the perfect Christian was to transcend (1 Cor. 7:1 to be read as a slogan of the Corinthian enthusiasts). The spiritual Christian was already now empowered to speak in tongues, the language spoken by angels in heaven (13:1; see also Luke 20:34–36). The possession of the spirit transports the higher class of Christians into an experience of liberation from physical bonds, and from forms of conduct enforced by obligations to communal life in the family, so that already existing marriages are dissolved to let the partners free for ecstatic experiences of their true selves (7:10–11). This search for freedom led some women in Corinth to manifest their liberation in ways that were meant to demonstrate the annulment of the differences between men and women. There is evidence from Jewish groups, but also from Greco-Roman backgrounds, that women cut their hair short and dressed like men because they wanted to display their refusal to be confined and defined by the characteristics of gender. In Christ, they argued, there is no longer male or female (see Gal. 3:28) and, therefore, worship was the appropriate place to show in public that being a man or a woman was inconsequential, even detrimental, to Christian freedom. The problem Paul is addressing in 1 Cor. 11:2–16 is, therefore, not primarily an issue of dress or haircut but the claim of an enthusiastic group that the distinction between men and women had to be abrogated, that the natural polarity of human existence in the differentiation of the sexes was inferior to the life in the spirit, and that the arrival of the new age cancelled out the reality of nature.

Some particularly telling evidence for this orientation can be found in the Gospel of Thomas. Logion 22 of the Gospel of Thomas preserves a version of Jesus' saying that one has to be like a child to enter the kingdom of God: "Jesus said to them, 'When you make the two one, and when you make the inside like the outside and the outside like the inside, and the above like the below, and when you make the male and the female one and the same, so that the male not be male nor the female female . . . then you will enter (the kingdom)'." Similar is logion 114 of the Gospel of Thomas: "Simon Peter said to them, 'Let Mary leave us, for women are not worthy of life.' Jesus said, 'I myself shall lead her in order to make her male, so that she too may become a living spirit resembling you males. For every woman who will make herself male will enter the kingdom of heaven'."

Paul's reply to this situation is shot through with appeals to the Old Testament creation stories. The male is not required to cover his head during worship because "he is the image and glory of God." This reasoning uses the sentence Gen. 1:27 about God's creation of the human being in God's image. The reference, however, is a loose one since the word "image" is expanded by the addition of "glory," which does not occur in the Old Testament verse but carries weight for Paul since he uses it again in the immediately ensuing statement "but woman is the glory of man." This is followed by the sentence "for man is not out of woman, but woman is out of man: because indeed man was not created for the sake of woman, but woman for the sake of man" (11:8–9). The echo of Genesis 2 is quite unmistakable. The Adam of this narrative is made by God from the dust of the ground, he is given the breath of life and becomes a living being (Gen. 2:7). The woman, however, is taken from Adam's side (Gen. 2:21–22), albeit Adam by himself is incomplete, in need of having a partner who is a part of his own being (Gen. 2:18 and 23).

It is very frequently assumed that Paul is defending a position that sets up the male as a superior creation of God in contradistinction to woman who is by nature dependent on the male. Not only 11:8–9 are interpreted in this way. The opening sentence of the whole argument, "the head of every man is Christ, the head of the woman is the man, and the head of Christ is God" (11:3) is understood to mean, in analogy to many Stoic and Jewish-Hellenistic parallels, an ontological hierarchy from God down to woman, who is at the lowest rung of the ladder; the statement "the man is the image and glory of God, but the woman is the glory of man" (11:7) is interpreted to imply that the male alone is created in the image of God. But this interpretation runs into great difficulties, especially because it cannot do justice to Paul's continuation of his own argument in 11:11–12: "In the Lord woman is not without man, nor man without woman. For just as woman is out of man, so is man through woman. And all this is out of God."

The word *head* in its metaphorical meaning in 11:3 does not mean "authority" or "overlord," but "origin" or "source," and the subjects said to be *head* do not form a chain from the highest to the lowest or from the lowest to the highest. Rather, in the sentence "the head of every man is Christ, the head of the woman is the man, and the head of Christ is God" (11:3), a sequence of ontological gradations is precisely not followed. Paul's interest lies in the establishment of relations in which the differences of male and female, of Christ and God are not nullified but understood as being essential components of a whole that is from God (11:12).

The intensive employment of the creation story in the context of a concrete situation in the gathering for worship in Corinth is intended to hold creation and redemption together. The new age, the life in faith, the possession of God's Spirit, do not cancel out what God has formed in creation. What is true "in the Lord" that "woman is not without man and man is not without woman" (11:12) is the reaffirmation of what is true in the act of creation, that "man is the image and glory of God and woman is the glory of man" (11:7). Far from denying the woman's participation in being— together with man—the image of God, the statement in 1 Cor. 11:7 attributes glory to both man and woman: Man is created to bring honor and praise to God, and woman is created to be the person whose existence draws honor and praise from the man.

Homosexuality: Rom. 1:18–32, especially vv. 23–27

Within the intense discussion about issues of homosexuality in recent years, this passage has received a great deal of fresh scrutiny, which in some respects has aided the clarification of some exegetical issues. Romans 1:18–32 contains no direct quotations from Genesis 1—2, and reliance on an Adam-typology as its background is not warranted. There are, however, clear allusions to God's creative act and to some phrases in Genesis 1 that are an important part of Paul's reasoning.

Romans 1:18–32 is the beginning of an extended argument leading to the conclusion that, in light of the revelation of God's power of salvation in the gospel (1:16–17), no human being will be justified in God's sight (3:20). Human life and history outside the rule of Moses' law is portrayed, as in an apocalyptic vision, like a mass of perdition that has rejected the knowledge of God, is caught in the primal sin of idolatry, and in consequence of that fatal error, manifests all kinds of moral perversion of which homosexual practices are highlighted as the most telling example (1:18–32). Yet in a sharp turn of argument that soon becomes clearly directed at those who acknowledge their allegiance to the Mosaic Torah, Jewish reliance on the saving efficacy of God's law is also demolished (2:1–3:30). The entire opening section of Romans is intended to lead to the conclusion that "there is no distinction, since all have sinned and fall short of the glory of God" (3:23–24), all persons are in need of God's gracious and unearned justification.

From the beginning of his argument against Gentile religion and morality in Rom. 1:18–32, Paul has in mind God as Creator, the cosmos as the creation of the invisible God, and Gentile religion as a fatally flawed attempt to seek in nature the manifestation of God. But the invisible God defies all images. "From the creation of the cosmos" (1:20) God's eternal power and godhead has been known. In spite of that knowledge, however, the Gentile world did not glorify and praise the true God but enmeshed themselves in futility by transforming the glory due to the Creator into the glorification of creatures: They "worshiped and served the creature rather than the Creator" (1:25).

In pursuing his argument Paul employs the rhetorical device of introducing a pair of interrelated concepts that are used three times in a row: the idea of *exchange* and the notion of "giving up." It is the term *exchange* that is, in our context, of great importance. Paul first states, as a general principle, the Jewish conviction that Gentile religion is idolatrous because it substitutes the honor due only to the immortal God for the veneration of images of mortal beings. Gentile religion "exchanged the glory of the immortal God for images resembling a mortal human being or birds or four-footed animals or reptiles" (1:23). Already in this first use of the idea of exchange, an allusion to the creation story in Genesis 1 is involved. The sequence "human being, birds, four-footed animals, and reptiles" echoes Gen. 1:26, which says that the human being is to have dominion over the fish of the sea, over the birds of the air, over the cattle, and over the reptiles. Paul's appeal to the Creator, and to creation, is not couched in abstract terms, as in our word *nature*. Rather, it is informed very concretely by the biblical creation story. Paul had learned what *Creator* and *creation* signify by the creation narratives at the beginning of Genesis, and the wording of these accounts provides him with the conceptuality of his argument.

The first exchange of legitimate for illegitimate worship is followed by a second one, in which for the first time in the passage the phrase "give up" also appears. The second exchange is not materially different from the first. Again it is said to consist in a transference of allegiance from a worthy subject to an object not worthy of veneration. Gentiles "exchanged the truth about God for a lie and worshiped and served the creature rather than the Creator" (1:25). But in this second step, the initial and fundamental exchange of loyalties is accompanied by a general but observable degradation in the bodies of those who practice idolatry (1:24). The phrase "degrading of their bodies" allows no specificity. In the third step involving the exchange, however, the specificity is palpable. The substitution of the honor due to the Creator with the religious reverence for mortal creatures leads, as a consequence, to a third exchange analogous to the first and second in that, again, a relationship established by the Creator is exchanged with another relationship that has no foundation in God's creation. "Women exchanged natural intercourse for unnatural, and in the same way also the men, giving up natural intercourse with women, were consumed with passion for one another" (1:26–27). Paul uses words for "men" and "women" in these verses that are otherwise not used in his letters (except in Gal. 3:28). The words derive from the vocabulary of the creation story in Gen. 1:27, where the one human being is said to exist in the form of the union of two, male and female. The three uses of the word *exchange* coordinate idolatrous religion and homosexual activity. Idolatrous religion substitutes the worship of the only true God for objects unworthy of veneration, and homosexuality substitutes the relationship established by the Creator with a relationship that has no foundation in God's creation. There is a precise analogy between the exchange of the Creator for creatures and the exchange of the Creator's act in ordaining the union of male and female for the union of members of the same sex.

Conclusion

On the basis of the observations above, seven conclusions may be warranted.

First, several of the most important New Testament passages dealing with issues of sexuality appeal to the creation stories in Genesis 1—2. This affirms that in the new creation—in the life of faith—sexuality is neither inconsequential nor abolished.

Second, it is striking that the same New Testament passages evoke the Creation story (Genesis 1—2) but never the account of the Fall (Genesis 3). Human sexuality is seen, in these texts, as a fundamental continuance of God's good creation. Actual sexual behavior, whether hetero- or homosexual, is subject to all kinds of perversions, and therefore sadly connected with the Fall. But being born male or female is the undiminished actuality of God's good creation.

Third, the New Testament passages discussed above deal with a wide variety of sexual questions: marriage and divorce, prostitution, gender differentiations in external appearance, and homosexuality. In all cases, the questions are decided by concentration on a single point: the creation of the one human form of life in the polarity of male and female. The distortion or abolition of this one crucial reality of being human is seen in the New Testament as an outrage against the Creator.

Fourth, all New Testament passages discussed above read the creation stories in Genesis 1—2 from a new vantage point. The Genesis narratives are now plunged into the light of the coming kingdom of God and of the justification of God in the work of Christ. This new understanding of the creation narratives intensifies the value of sexual life, and heightens the demand expected in sexual behavior. The criticism of divorce and the rejection of prostitution go beyond Old Testament law, and the radicality of perceiving homosexuality as an outcome of idolatry projects Old Testament legislation onto the screen of apocalyptic disaster.

Fifth, the sections we studied contain without exception ethical mandates, or at least strong directives, for sexual conduct. But they are also without exception mindful of a creational ontology that is given in the word form of the narratives of Genesis 1—2. Being male or female is a reality prior to law and morality, and prior to individual choices. A point often made in the modern debate about homosexuality in the church is the observation that Old and New Testament had no knowledge of the difference between a homosexual orientation and homosexual acts engaged in by heterosexually oriented people. The observation is correct but it misses the point. The notion of sexual orientation, or sexual preference, is based on the individualistic idea that sexuality is determined by personal inclination or choice: What individual desire dictates is the decisive norm for sexual conduct. Biblical sexual ethos is irreconcilable with this individualistic approach. The biblical view of human sexuality as the union between male and female posits a relationship with all its consequences as the core of sexual relations. Part of these consequences is the lifelong acceptance of the gift and the challenge of the other, the procreation and rearing of children and the care for the family. This means human sexuality is, as God's creation of male and female, bound up with community and, therefore, with unselfish service, with discipline, and with the will to subordinate individual desires, including sexual urges, to the well-being of others.

Sixth, it is a fundamental mistake to discuss biblical statements on homosexuality in isolation from the positive ethos of human sexuality in scripture. As bits and pieces of Old Testament legislation, and of Jewish heritage in the New Testament, the sparse references to homosexuality could well be attributed to the social conditions of a distant past. But seen against the foil of the extremely high valuation given to the counterpoint of maleness and femaleness in God's creation in the Bible, the sole attribution to time-bound modes of social norms cannot be maintained. On the background of the positive ethos of human sexuality in Old and New Testament, homosexuality becomes inescapably a denial of the goodness of God's creation.

Seventh, the consideration above of the indebtedness of some New Testament teaching to the Old Testament creation stories can also leave no doubt that nobody in the Christian community occupies a place of achievement that would allow exemption from the searing criticism of sexual mores found in the New Testament. But we would be ill served, in discussions on homosexuality, divorce, obsession with sex, widespread promiscuity, or any other aspect of sexual behavior, to encapsulate ourselves in the dictates of contemporary cultural trends and the presumed necessities of our modern insights, to the neglect of the voice of the New Testament (and the Old Testament with it) that proclaims the ever-challenging, ever-liberating, distant glory of God's creation of the human as male and female.

Part 2

*How Do the Scriptures Inform
Our Theological Reflection?*

5

What the Scriptures Principally Teach

Patrick D. Miller

What the biblical texts say about homosexuality is a matter of some debate. But the larger issue for discussion is less about what the texts say than it is about what we do with that, how we take the textual material as a guide or direction for thinking and acting about sexual relations. Indeed, the church's debate about homosexuality is a particular and significant piece of an ongoing discussion about sexual relationships and ethics and the role that traditional Christian perspectives, shaped by a long history of interpreting scripture, play in determining how Christians should and do behave, which are not necessarily the same thing. In what follows, I will suggest issues that seem appropriate to our discussion of how the church is to regard homosexual conduct and what place persons who engage in same-sex activity have in the community of faith.

The Teaching of Scripture

There is not much biblical direction on the matter of homosexuality. Only in the Holiness Code of Leviticus (18:22 and 20:13) do we have actual directives or commands, that is, formal instruction about same-sex conduct. In both instances, sexual relations with a person of the same sex is prohibited in the context of other prohibitions of unacceptable sexual relationships. In the New Testament, the topic comes up primarily in lists of vices that are enumerated in the context of some other topic, for example, lawsuits (1 Cor. 6:9), the proper use of the law (1 Tim. 1:10), and Paul's argument in Rom. 1:26–27 about the corruption of human nature as testified to in various forms of immorality that are outgrowths of idolatry (homosexual activity being one of these). There is some serious debate among New Testament scholars about how to read the New Testament texts and how explicitly homosexual activity as we customarily think of it is in view.[1] But even if one assumes that the texts do indeed speak of same-sex relationships as we customarily think of them, there is not much to build upon here in terms of direct address of the topic. Two things are clear from the merest review of the direct evidence of scripture: Homosexual relationships are not at all to the fore in scripture, but to whatever extent they are discussed, they are condemned as unacceptable, abominable, or wicked.

In terms of indirect scriptural guidance, one may cite the creation story in Genesis 1—3 where male-female relationships are addressed. From this, one might infer something about what is fitting and proper for sexual activity.

With reference to both kinds of evidence, the Old Testament illustrates the elusiveness of the biblical material and the difficulty of reading instruction directly from it. The believing reader of the laws of the Old Testament is met by a kind of dialectic or tension that cannot be dissolved easily and is discernible in a close look at the laws, their order, sequence, and interrelationships. The present shape of the law, as well as what we can discern of its formation, point us to a dual reality—a core of perduring, foundational law or instruction and a congeries of specifics or particularities of that foundational law that are worked out over the passage of time and changing circumstance. The "core" is clearly the Decalogue, or Ten Commandments. The commandments have been placed first in both accounts of the revelation of the law at Sinai (Ex. 19:1—Num. 10:10; Deuteronomy 5). They are essentially the same in both formulations.[2] The Ten Commandments are explicitly separated from the rest of the Torah, and both Exodus 20 and Deuteronomy 5 give an account of that separation, reporting that the Decalogue was given directly to the people while the rest of the legal material was given by God to Moses for him to teach to the people. In other words, the very shape and formation of the laws of the Old Testament mark out the Ten Commandments as foundational and unchanging, the touchstone to which all other laws are to be connected—enduring, adaptable, and effective for life in all situations.

The rest of the law is specific in spelling out these commandments. That is not always self-evident; nor can one say that it was always the motivation behind the law. But, especially in Deuteronomy, it is possible to see that the rest of the specific laws are arranged in the order of the Decalogue as an elaboration of its force in particular details and precedents.[3] That means we can seriously look at and draw upon the rest of the law for guidance in understanding the fundamental instruction of the Lord as given to us in the Decalogue.

But none of the specifics have the force of the original. They have themselves arisen in different times and under different circumstances, so that the specifications of Deuteronomy are not necessarily like those of Exodus 21—23[4] and neither of those legal codes are the same as those of Leviticus and Numbers, themselves composed of more than one set of Torah instructions.[5]

The present form of the Torah materials of the Old Testament, therefore, present us with several implications for the way we receive and attend to the divine revelation therein. There is clearly a basic law, the Decalogue, that continues the same and is the primary obligation for the community that lives in obedience to this God. There are many specific laws that help us see some of the particulars of the basic obligations. They are instructive but not necessarily obligatory in the same fashion. In some instances, they have high moral impact upon the contemporary community of faith without being carried out; for example, the gleaning laws and the laws of sabbatical and jubilee release (Leviticus 25 and Deuteronomy 15). In other cases, even in laws that are formulated—like the Decalogue—in apodictic or prohibitive fashion, the contemporary community of faith does not find the particular specification as binding or morally desirable. So many cases of these are found in Leviticus and Deuteronomy that there is little need to list them here.[6] These specific formulations help us see in particular times (though we are not always sure exactly what those times were) how the primary obligations were spelled out. The laws of Leviticus 18 and 20 in some sense represent a move from the commandment against adultery into the whole sphere of sexual relationships and the seriousness of these. There is much that we can and do learn from that. But these laws do not bind in a different fashion than other Levitical laws that we have set aside in practice. One cannot simply read from the two prohibitions in Leviticus 18 and 20 a final and binding moral word about same-sex relationships in the same way that one can read a final word from the prohibition against adultery in the Decalogue, though those prohibitions, along with others in the lists, can be instructive for developing an ethic of sexual relationships.[7]

So in our moral deliberation, we are, like the earlier community of faith at different times in its history, faced with having to determine what God wills of us in our time and how the fundamental guidelines work out in specifics today. That process has been going on throughout the history of the church. For example, restrictions on who may be ordained that were operative in the Levitical laws and in later times are no longer operative in our time. We have decided on various grounds—theological, moral, pragmatic, and the like—that the specifics of the law of the Old Testament no longer bind us and restrict who may be ordained. In our own time and context, we have to work out the specifics of obedience to the fundamental commands.

The earlier specifications are not to be ignored. They continue to be instructive, though they vary considerably in the degree to which we pay attention to them. What is clear is that we do not place them all on the same level, even as time-specific reflections of the basic commands of the Decalogue. One can point rather easily to spheres of conduct in which the church has made a different moral judgment than that found in specific texts of the Bible. Scripture permits some things to which we say "no"—most obviously slavery and male domination of women. We are convinced that our restriction of scripture's apparent permission is faithful to the gospel and, indeed, is ultimately directed by what we have learned from scripture. Scripture also prohibits many things that we permit. The laws of the Old Testament are full of examples. But in the case of divorce, for example, the church has interpreted scripture against scripture—even against the very specific words of Jesus—to permit divorce and remarriage after divorce.

The *indirect* evidence of the Old Testament relevant to the sexual relationship between different and same sexes is found especially in the picture of the created order as encountered in Genesis 1—3. That depiction clearly joins man and woman together in responsibility for filling and ruling the earth, for procreating and controlling God's creation. The image of God is found in the human being as male and female. I take that Genesis story very seriously. But here, in these chapters, is one of the places where in some sense we say no to what we hear in scripture and do so in the light of our whole understanding of scripture. I am speaking particularly of the divine judgment in Genesis 3. The history of the church and of the larger society is one of resistance to the circumstances announced by God as outcomes of the human sin recounted in Genesis 3. We do everything we can to overcome the pain and travail of childbirth. In like manner, much of the economic history of the human race, a history much supported and influenced by the church, has been an effort to overcome or reduce the pain and toil of human labor to feed ourselves—to make it easier to extract bread from the earth. Such efforts are generally judged as morally very positive, except as they represent actions that lead to oppression of others. And finally, in our own time, we are making much headway in overcoming the subordination of female to male, of wife to husband, that is announced also in Genesis 3. We do not take these etiologies of the human condition, which place their causality in the divine sentence of judgment, as normative. That is because of the larger scriptural conviction that God moves to deal graciously with us and offers us possibilities of life that do not depend upon pain and anxious labor. We also do not take them as normative because of the other words of scripture and of God that set man and woman together to rule the creation.

Indeed, often it is where scripture seems to fix the way relationships must be and roles must be set—woman subordinate to man, man to cut his hair and woman not to, woman not to speak out in the church, slaves to be submissive to their masters and obey them in fear and trembling as they obey Christ—that the church has heard in the gospel and in the prophetic and liberating words of both Old Testament and New Testament a counter word that does not fix people in roles and relationships and does not let cultural and social mores in this regard become final definitions of who and what we are in the church and the kingdom.

The Genesis stories picture an ideal of enduring companionship of man and woman—one that has sexual relationship for procreation—as central to the human story.[8] That tells us something very fundamental about who and what we are. The defining relationship in the human community is man and woman. That relationship often is manifest in the establishment of a commitment between a man and a woman that perdures and is fruitful in every respect. Of course, for many human beings that particular ideal is not their experience. They may be single and so do not know the man–woman relationship as one of enduring and intimate companionship, sexual and otherwise (or at least not necessarily so). They may be barren and so do not know the procreative fruit of the relationship that God intends. They may be homosexual and so do not know the experience of existing in sexual relationship with a companion of opposite gender. Yet all of these persons, whose numbers are legion, are truly members of the human community God has made and of the community of faith. As persons who in their varied ways and relationships live out lives of service to God, lives of faithfulness, love, and justice, caring for one another and loving God, their place in the community of faith and my judgment of them are not determined by their roles and relationships.

In his final and posthumous work, Paul Lehmann acutely perceived the different possibilities for receiving and drawing upon the Genesis account of the creation of man and woman. His comments are indicative of the fact that what the text says does not yet tell us what it teaches; that happens only when the text is perceived from some angle of vision. For Lehmann, as it should be for us all, that angle was the gospel, which is, in his now-familiar formulation, what God was and is doing to make and to keep human life human. That definition of God's work in the world is particularly apropos for this issue, and Lehmann's angle on the Genesis account is worth citing:

> [A] divine ordination is not a *limiting* instance, but a *foundational* one. As a limiting instance, the divine ordination to sexual otherness and reciprocity is put forward as the normative mode of sexuality, in relation to which variants are excluded as deviants from the heterosexual norm. As a *foundational* instance, the divine ordination to sexual otherness and reciprocity becomes the liberating instance in relation to which divergent possibilities may be pursued and assessed. As a *limiting* instance, heterosexuality necessarily excludes homosexuality from the divine purpose of and for human fulfillment. As a *foundational* instance of otherness in differentiation and commitment, inequality and heterogeneity, reciprocity and fidelity, heterosexuality becomes the liberating occasion and sign of human fulfillment in relation to which homosexuality may also be affirmed. Just as in Scripture and tradition, a central and indispensable correlation between monotheism and monogamy has been discerned and affirmed, yet without requiring the

instantaneous and intransigent rejection of concubinage, poly-
andry or polygamy, or even interracial and/or interfaith marriage
as a test case of the obedience of faith, so the foundational and liberating instance of heterosexuality as a parable of human fulfillment does not require an intransigent rejection of homosexuality
as a test case of the obedience of faith.[9]

The Rule of Faith and Love

Interpretation of scripture in the church should not happen without attention to the rule of faith and the rule of love. The former suggests that
our individual interpretations are placed against the community's understanding of scripture in past and present. In the Reformed community, that
interpretive backdrop is found particularly in the creeds and confessions,
though not only there. The subject of homosexuality has not been a specific focus of attention in these documents, though the Heidelberg Catechism quotes 1 Cor. 6:9 in one of its questions and interprets homosexuality as one of the sins that keeps one from inheriting the kingdom of God.
The tradition thus places the present interpreter in a kind of tension. On
the one hand, there is inattention to the issue; on the other hand, where the
tradition has dealt with the matter in or out of the confessions, it has generally condemned the practice of same-sex activity. In that context, it is important that the present interpretive activity of the church be a communal
one, that our efforts to think about this issue afresh and in reference to what
has been thought already be a corporate engagement and not simply a matter of individual proposals for reading texts, although we may start at that
point. Our interpretation happens in community, and what the community
experiences in faith is more significant than the experience of any individual. What we say and do together is more to be attended to than idiosyncratic readings of texts by one or a few individuals. This means listening to
a broad range of interpretive judgments in the church, including its gay and
lesbian members.

Thus, one of the tasks of the church today is to seek the guidance of the
Holy Spirit in reading these texts. The rule of faith has made us reluctant
to view same-sex activity as other than a sinful mark, but neither scripture
nor the confessions has lifted this topic up for major attention. The very
struggle of the church—the large attention that homosexual practice is receiving in the moral, theological, and interpretive discussions of the
church—indicates that the rule of faith is properly under scrutiny and that
the church is listening for direction from the Holy Spirit. The rule of faith
is not fixed, but it is also not changed by any individual. It is my sense that
in the matter before us, faith is rethinking its understanding and is attentive to both what the church has said in the past and also what it is thinking and saying now. The Scots Confession says this: "We dare not receive

or admit any interpretation which is contrary to any principal point of our faith, or to any other plain text of scripture, or to the rule of love" (chapter 18). It is the phrase "any other plain text of scripture," that appears to give us undebatable clarity on how we judge homosexuality, but the other criteria of the Scots Confession may take us in other directions. We are not, in fact, dealing with "any principal point of our faith" in this regard, and we may be in significant conflict with the rule of love as a guide to how we read and respond to the scriptures.

That rule of love reminds us that our interpretation of scripture stands under the divine command to love God and neighbor. Thus, what we hear from scripture should not lead us away from the expression of love for others. Or, in the words of the document "Presbyterian Understanding and Use of Holy Scripture," adopted by the General Assembly of the Presbyterian Church (U.S.A.) in 1983,

> all interpretations are to be judged by the question whether they offer and support the love given and commanded by God. When interpretations do not meet this criterion, it must be asked whether the text has been used correctly in the light of the whole Scripture and its subject.[10]

One of the classic Reformed statements, that of the Synod of Berne in 1528, puts it this way:

> But where something is brought before us by our pastors or others, which brings us closer to Christ, and in accordance with God's Word is more conducive to mutual friendship and Christian love than the interpretation now presented, we will gladly accept it. . .[11]

The interpretive comment of the "Presbyterian Understanding . . . of Holy Scripture" statement at this point is very revealing, particularly in light of the fact that it was not written with any reference to the church's hermeneutical debate about the appropriate regard and judgment of persons who engage in same-sex love. That document says:

> No interpretation of Scripture is correct that leads to or supports contempt for any individual or group of persons either within or outside of the church. Such results from the interpretation of Scripture plainly indicate that the rule of love has not been honored.[12]

To the extent that such a test of our interpretation by the rule of love can be made, the church has fallen far short in its use of the texts dealing with homosexuality. Our record on this is all too clear. Exceptions are notable, but the history is generally one of the church's rejection and contempt of those identified by themselves or others as gay and lesbian. It is not simply that we have precluded their holding positions of leadership, which indeed we have done, but we have not welcomed them fully into the fellowship of the church. And the church by its influence and the power of its religious character has been complicit, sometimes in very open fashion, in the larger oppression of homosexual persons by society. Our judgment that homosexual activity is a sin has controlled the way we have behaved toward Christians who are homosexual.[13] The rule of love, which says that our interpretation is correlative with the way we live, raises serious questions about what we have done with the plain sense of scripture. If it is a means by which we inflict pain and put down other Christians—or other human beings of any stripe—then our interpretation is under question.

At this point, then, one needs to ask about the preeminence of the gospel and of the grace of God as a guide for our proper response to scripture. That response may not be the same as what the plain sense of some texts would indicate. We are not to lose sense, however, of what it is that "the Scriptures principally teach," as the Catechism puts it.[14] The *answer* to that question is what we are to believe concerning God and what duty God requires of us. It is no accident that the verses undergirding this answer that are cited in the scripture proofs accompanying the Westminster documents are Micah 6:8, John 3:16, and John 20:31. These are fundamental formulations of the gospel, of the love of God revealed in Jesus Christ, and of our responsibility to "do justice and love kindness and walk humbly with your God." It is precisely the manifestation of justice and kindness that in this, as in all instances, is a fundamental criterion of our interpretation of scripture. What is ultimately at stake is the triumph of grace in the church.

Knowledge and Experience

Finally, a word needs to be said about the place of knowledge and experience. In another chapter in this volume, Choon-Leong Seow properly calls attention to scripture's own acknowledgment that we learn the way of obedience and love, at least in part, by means of our experience and new knowledge that is gained from it. The way of human discernment and reason's sensibility in the light of the complexities we encounter is not something foreign to scripture or disdained by scripture in favor of a simple reading of texts. It is scripture itself that teaches us the importance of new knowledge, of the investigation of science, of the proven wisdom that comes from experience and is a part of our fear of the Lord. We tend to set the revelation of scripture condemning homosexual acts against our human desire to be open to the homosexual person and against our sense from experience that homosexuality is not finally reducible simply to the category of sin. But that tendency to trump experience with revelation comes up against scripture's own valuing of the wisdom of experience and its insistence that those who fear the Lord are to take account of what knowledge and wisdom teach us.

Such learning from experience is not meant to be idiosyncratic; that is, experience is a shared phenomenon, something that each of us gains individually but that belongs to a body of learned knowledge checked and confirmed by the experience of others. Nevertheless, experience, by definition, is something that comes to us out of the living of our lives and what we learn from the living that others have done.

I cannot avoid a personal word about my own experience regarding this point. My construal of scripture and my response, both theologically and practically, to this and other issues is strongly shaped by the experience of growing up in the southern United States between 1930 and 1960, in an ethos in which persons were excluded from normal participation in the society—church or otherwise—because of who they were. The fundamental wrongness of that exclusion, the terrible sin that we committed in perpetuating that exclusion in a segregated society and a segregated church, has made me forever question any moves in church and society that judge and exclude persons for who they are and rule them out of full acceptance and participation. The church has a long history of similar sinful activity for which it is accountable in excluding from acceptance and loving attention those who are homosexual. That personal experience has thus stamped me in a certain way, affecting how I deal with this issue. I am willing to let my experience, which is shared by many other Christians, and the conclusions I draw from it be criticized and to listen to those who would do so. But I cannot fail to be affected and shaped by my experience. For me, it is no less than the power of the gospel in the church that is at stake.

NOTES

1. There is much discussion about what forms of sexual activity may be in view in the biblical texts under consideration—pederasty, male prostitution, heterosexual participation in homosexual acts, homosexuality in general, male, female, or whatever.
2. The differences between the formulations of the Decalogue in Exodus 20 and Deuteronomy 5 are relatively minor when compared with differences in the rest of the laws where parallels of some sort exist. The primary difference is in the formulation of the sabbath commandment, where Exodus and Deuteronomy give different motivations for keeping the commandments. Other deuteronomic stylistic features are present in Deuteronomy 5.
3. In the Holiness Code, for example, one of the prohibitions of same-sex relationships is placed in a series that begins by reiterating the commandment against adultery, suggesting that the series is to be seen in relation to that commandment (Lev. 20:10ff).
4. For a succinct presentation of the parallel material in Exodus 21—23 (the Book of the Covenant) and Deuteronomy 12—26, together with some discussion of how these collections seem to represent different stages in the

life and economic history of the Israelite community, see G. von Rad, *Deuteronomy* in The Old Testament Library (Philadelphia: Westminster Press, 1966), 12–15. On the relationship of the various bodies of legal material to one another, see F. Crüsemann, *Die Tora: Theologie und Sozialgeschichte des altestamentlichen Gesetzes* (München: Kaiser, 1992), to appear in English as *The Torah: The Theology and Social History of Laws in the Hebrew Bible* (Minneapolis: Fortress Press, forthcoming).

5. For the most recent detailed proposal concerning the character and setting of the different collections of legal material in Leviticus and Numbers, see Israel Knohl, *The Sanctuary of Silence: The Priestly Torah and the Holiness School* (Minneapolis: Fortress Press, 1995).

6. For examples, see the chapter by C.-L. Seow in this volume.

7. There is a long history in the church of seeking to distinguish between laws that were seen as binding and those that were not. Various approaches may be discerned in that history. Acts 15 seems to indicate a difference between Jewish Christians who kept the whole of the law (v. 5) and gentile Christians who were expected to maintain certain abstentions identified in the law (v. 20). In the second century, Christian polemic against the Jews maintained that the laws given after the incident of the golden calf were only binding upon a disobedient Israel, that is, the Jews (I am indebted to Dean McBride for calling this to my attention). Calvin identified the moral law with the Decalogue and Jesus' summary of it and saw it as the fundamental law clearly applicable to Christians. This moral law was the most important, but other laws functioned in relation to it in different ways. Some of the law he saw as precepts "which are not found in the Two Tables, yet differ not at all from them in sense; so that due care must be taken to afix them to their respective Commandments in order to present the Law as a whole." In addition to these, there were "supplements." He explain the "supplements" as follows:

. . . with respect to the First Table, the Ceremonies and the outward Exercises of Worship; with respect to the Second Table, the Political laws, for the object of both these parts is merely to aid in the observance of the Moral Law; and it is not a little important, that we should understand that the Ceremonies and the Judicial Ordinances neither change nor detract from the rule laid down in the Ten Commandments; but are only helps, which as it were lead us by the hand to the due Worship of God, and to the promotion of justice towards men.

. . . therefore it follows, that nothing can be wanted as the rule of a good and upright life beyond the Ten Commandments. (J. Calvin, *Commentaries on the Four Last Books of Moses, Arranged in the Form of a Harmony* [Edinburgh: The Calvin Translation Society, 1852], 1: xvi–xvii).

Interestingly, Calvin puts the homosexuality laws of Leviticus 18 and 20 only in the supplements, and in one case in the "political supplements." He associated them with the commandment against adultery as further prohibitions against "all sins which are repugnant to the modesty of nature itself" (3:73). There is no doubt that he thought these directives were guides for the Christian life.

8. This is not, by the way, the ideal that Paul sets forth for the Christian community.

9. P. Lehmann, *The Decalogue and a Human Future: The Meaning of the Commandments for Making and Keeping Human Life Human* (Grand Rapids: Wm. B. Eerdmans Publishing Co., 1995), 174. The completion and publication of this work is due significantly to the labors of Nancy Duff, whose introduction is helpful for understanding Lehmann's perspective on law and commandment.

10. "Presbyterian Understanding and Use of Holy Scripture" (Louisville Ky.: The Office of the General Assembly, 1992), 19–20.

11. Quoted in "Presbyterian Understanding and Use of Holy Scripture," 20.

12. Ibid., 20

13. The phrase "who are homosexual" implicitly introduces the large and much discussed question of whether or not homosexuality is at all genetic, a trait of being and personhood in some sense, or only a practice that is adopted and can be set aside, even with difficulty. However that discussion moves— and it is dependent upon all sorts of continuing studies and varying anthropologies—there is no doubt that many homosexual Christians have found their homosexuality something that is a part of them, and in some cases, would gladly have given it up if they could, if for no other reason than the hostility of church and society toward them. Staying "in the closet" is an act of those who protect themselves from a pain that other Christians have and do inflict, in no small measure because of how we have read and followed scripture.

14. "The Westminster Shorter Catechism," Question 3.

6

Living with the Bible

Thomas G. Long

"Duncan Henderson grew up on a wheat farm, walked two miles to school every day and always believed he could find answers in the Bible." So begins an article in *The Wall Street Journal* about the Henderson family of Jennings, Missouri, a narrative of faith and courage in the midst of suffering.[1]

In the spring of 1973, Paul Henderson, twenty-six years old and the only child of Duncan and Virginia Henderson, announced to his parents that he had a confession to make. "I haven't really been honest with you," he said. "I'm gay." The Hendersons were modest, traditional people. Duncan worked at the Missouri Portland Cement Company and was an elder in the local Presbyterian church in Jennings. Virginia taught kindergarten and sang in the choir. Paul's birth was one of the couple's fondest memories. The news that Virginia had gone into labor came to Duncan as he was mopping floors at his Sears job, and he threw down the mop and raced to catch a bus to the hospital. "I was real pleased," he said, remembering that day, "to have a son."

Now that same son was telling him something that shook his world. As far as Duncan knew, he had never met a gay person in his life; indeed, he had always considered homosexuality a sin. His son's secret staggered him, left him silent. Finally, he managed, haltingly, to rise. Duncan embraced Paul and said, "You're our son and we love you."

Paul was a graduate of Westminster College, a Presbyterian school in Fulton, Missouri. Feeling called into the ministry during his college years, he had gone from Westminster to McCormick Theological Seminary, where he enrolled in a combined M.Div. and M.S.W. program. As a ministerial candidate in 1976, however, Paul told presbytery officials the truth about himself, and the church, embroiled in a debate about homosexuality and ordination, rejected his ministerial candidacy. Duncan was hurt by what his church did toward his son. "We'd always gone to church," he said. "We'd always been generous with our money, and here they were being heavy-handed. Paul was never a problem. . . . Still, they wouldn't have anything to do with him."

The doorway to ministry closed, Paul become a social worker in Chicago and was active in the effort to open Chicago House, a hospice for AIDS patients, never imagining that he would someday need the services of this hospice himself. However, nearly sixteen years after he first told his parents of his homosexuality, Paul was admitted to a Chicago emergency room with pneumonia. The worst was true, and he phoned his parents back in Missouri with words even more numbing, even more difficult to hear than his earlier revelation, "I got some test results back today. I have AIDS."

"You grow old," Duncan thought when the news took hold. "You think your children are going to take care of you. But we will be burying Paul." That night, Duncan cried himself to sleep. The next day, Duncan and Virginia drove the six hours to Chicago to be with Paul, the first of many such trips over the next few months. When the travel between Jennings and Chicago began to wear on the Hendersons, who were now in their seventies, they sold their home in Jennings and moved in with Paul and began to care for him around the clock.

For three years, the Hendersons nursed their son, worked to ensure that he received hospice care, and joined a support group for friends and relatives of AIDS sufferers. Paul's parents agonized with him, and through their suffering, became stronger, deeper people. One Sunday after church, Paul was astonished to hear his traditional midwestern mother go up to a person she barely knew, a gay man whose companion had died of AIDS, and say, "I know how you feel."

On the morning of his seventy-fifth birthday, Duncan woke early and began to read the Bible. He remembers that his eyes fell on a passage from James promising that fervent prayer brings the blessing of healing. But the healing that came in the waning weeks of Paul's life was not a bodily kind; it was in the relationship between father and son. Paul and Duncan, once formal and somewhat distant, drew close, became loving and trusting. "As the years go by," Duncan said later, "I will always be grateful that I went up there and took care of him."

On October 10, 1991, the end came. For five and a half hours Paul gasped for air as Duncan and Virginia took turns holding his hand. When Paul's exhausted and diminished body finally yielded, Duncan placed his arms around his wife, and, for the first time since Paul told them he was sick, they wept together.

Hearing the Bible in Congregational Context

For the Hendersons, scripture and suffering, Christianity and homosexuality, faith and AIDS, congregational life and personal heartache came together. At one level, their story is remarkable, a moving amalgam of pathos and grace, courage and forgiveness. At another level, though, what is most remarkable about the Hendersons is that their experience is unremarkable, that it is unexceptional. In 1992, when the article first appeared, *The Wall Street Journal* may have been intrigued by the angle of a middle-class American family struggling toward dignity and mercy in the face of what many would have defined as a Greenwich Village problem, but most pastors know better. Some version of the Hendersons' story is being lived out in virtually every Christian congregation across the land.

I would like to think about the role of the Bible in relationship to the circumstances of church people like the Hendersons. More specifically, I want to explore one of the main themes of this volume—the Bible and homosexuality—not primarily as an exegetical, historical, systematic theological, or ethical concern (those approaches are important, and others will explore them far more ably than I can) but as a matter of congregational hermeneutics. What difference does it make that the Hendersons are mainstream Christians, that their exposure to the Bible and the faith was not over the radio, in secret mystical illuminations, in a card box full of "precious promises" on the kitchen table, but in the preaching, teaching, and worship of a typical American congregation? I want to imagine myself (and to invite you to do the same) as the pastor of the Hendersons, as the minister of their Presbyterian congregation in Jennings or one like it, as the one who must preach and teach and interpret the scripture in the community of faith where such people worship and serve, and I want to inquire about how this environment affects the impact of scripture on an issue like homosexuality.

I do this not as an act of intrusion or presumption, even in the arena of the imagination, and certainly not in order to use actual people and their real pain as some sort of simulation exercise, a playful test case. I do not know the Hendersons, though I believe that I know many others like them. I am allowing their circumstances to form the framework of this discussion in order to raise the stakes, to ground the work of biblical interpretation in a particular and concrete actuality, to place the task of biblical discernment in the context of a Christian congregation with its specific mission, constraints, and lines of accountability.

I am persuaded that both the process and the results of discerning scripture on an urgent and complex issue like homosexuality are profoundly affected when the Bible is interpreted in the middle of the rough-and-tumble world of real congregational life. By this, I am not suggesting that biblical interpretation somehow becomes better, more real, or more "practical" (versus "theoretical") when it moves into the environment of the church. Nor am I saying that biblical interpretation needs somehow to wrest itself free from the high-altitude debates of the theological academy and the biblical guild and to resettle in the valley of the actual church and human life. It is, of course, current sport to attack seminaries and their faculties for overspecialization and alienation from the "real world" of the parish church. There is a measure of truth here, of course, and a necessary point can be made about this estrangement between parish and seminary, but that is not *my* point. Indeed, much that passes for sharp critique of seminaries is finally a witch's brew of sheer nostalgia, a flawed vision of theological pedagogy, a manifestation of the latent antiintellectualism that prowls its way through American culture, a serious misconception about the discrete missions of school and church, and a grievous underestimation of the churchly commitments countless seminary professors possess.[2]

What I *am* saying is that a worshiping, serving, learning, growing Christian congregation is a unique environment for biblical interpretation and that this environment influences the possibilities for biblical understanding. The church—namely, a congregation with people like Duncan, Virginia, and Paul Henderson in its ranks—is not a more authentic place to do biblical interpretation than the academy, but it is a different place, and seeking to understand scripture in the context of a congregation yields different results.

The issue is not theory versus practice, or sophisticated approaches to hermeneutics versus rough-hewn methods. Each environment—church and academy—employs its own intricate strategies and its own complex array of interpretive skills to make sense of the text. The key issue, broadly put, as Charles Wood among others has so ably argued, is *use;* Christian congregations, balancing pastoral care and mission, fellowship and service, stewardship and worship, theological confessions and baptismal promises, simply use the Bible in ways different from the public at large or the academy—even the seminary version of the academy—and use profoundly affects understanding.

A cab driver and a cartographer, claims Wood, look at the same map, but arrive at somewhat different understandings. It is not that one is an expert and the other a laborer. Each is a specialist of sorts, and their varying understandings are functions of their differing uses of the text. Wood goes on to state:

> What constitutes understanding depends a great deal on the use one wants to make of the text, as well as on the character of the text itself. The varied understandings of which a given text is patient cannot always be ordered on a scale from greater to less; they may simply be different. . . . The historian and the believer may cultivate differing abilities with regard to the same scripture material because each has a different use to make of it, and these two understandings might not compete or conflict. (Then again, they might, in a particular instance. There are likely to be complex relationships and interdependences among such uses.)[3]

I want to think, therefore, about how congregations put the Bible to use in regard to an issue like homosexuality. My goal is not at all to set forth a "biblical" or a "Christian" position on the matter of homosexuality, even a congregationally nuanced one. I have my own rather complex and evolving views on these matters, but they are just that—my views. Despite countless statements and pronouncements, the larger church is probably not prepared to render a finished judgment on the matter of homosexuality. Indeed, part of my point will be to raise questions about the possibility of such a fixed view, to argue that the larger and worthy doctrinal goal of discerning Christian truth, believed everywhere and by all, must be nuanced by the inescapably local and congregational character of Christianity. On the horizon is the cathedral of God's truth, and we are all making pilgrimage toward it. For the time being, though, along the pilgrim path, the biblical mandate for the congregations of Galatia or Grand Rapids may not be what is biblical for the congregation at Corinth or at Jennings, Missouri. My goal, therefore, will not be to create yet another theological position on homosexuality, but to name some of the constraints and conditions that prevail when congregationally based Christians try to live with the Bible, to say something of what happens when the Bible is read, discerned, and obeyed in congregational context.

Living Together with the Bible

When the Bible is interpreted in a seminary classroom or in a seminar of the Society of Biblical Literature, certain goals, methods, and rules of procedure prevail. These standards are not alien to congregational life—in their own ways, congregations care about matters like grammar, historical veracity, and relationship between texts just as much as the Society of Biblical Literature—but the prevailing conditions and norms for biblical interpretation are significantly modified in a worshiping, working Christian congregation.

The list is potentially long and quite complex, but here are a few observations about some of these congregational constraints on biblical interpretation:

A congregationally based process of biblical inquiry unsettles any notion of strict analogy in connecting text and context. One way in which the Bible is typically brought to bear on contemporary ethical matters is through analogy, a logical ratio proposed between some situation in a biblical text and a corresponding circumstance in the contemporary context. The analogy can be clumsy ("yes, aren't we today in our cities just like Sodom?") or more sophisticated ("the church's challenge to be open to homosexuals today is much like the early church's challenge to accept gentiles"), but whether it appears in naive or polished form, the analogy depends upon a certain alleged fixed symmetry between text and context.

However, the more one becomes immersed in congregational life, the more one is impressed not only with the constant themes in the human condition but also with the peculiarities of any given human situation. One recognizes the dissimilarities, the uniqueness, the unrepeatable aspects of every circumstance. To be specific, there is much about Paul Henderson's story as a homosexual that is familiar. His awareness in his early teens that he was somehow different from other boys, his strong teenage crushes and attraction to other males, his first homosexual encounter in college, his fleeing to the big city to explore an alternative lifestyle—there is much here that represents a recognizable pattern when viewed from sufficient distance.

But when Paul's life is viewed not through the wide-angled lens of cultural patterns and sociological trends but through the high-powered lens of baptismal accountability, pastoral guidance, and congregational *koinonia*, a different picture emerges. This is no statistical trend; this is Paul Henderson, child of the covenant. His life is no collection of social probabilities; he is a collection of improbabilities, his life an arena where the congregation expects to see the surprising grace of God at work. The more we are genuinely responsive to our baptismal vows toward him, the more we seek to understand him, his family life, even his homosexuality, both in terms of his own self-understanding and his behavior with others, and the more we would be forced to acknowledge the distinctiveness of his life. He fits no pattern with precision, not even a biblical one. His life is unparalleled even by any situation countenanced in scripture.

William Placher makes this point in thinking through the relationship to contemporary culture of two Old Testament texts—Lev. 18:22 ("You shall not lie with a male as with a woman; it is an abomination") and Lev. 20:13 ("If a man lies with a male as with a woman, both of them have committed an abomination"):

> If two men in the contemporary United States (notice that the Levitical passages do not refer to lesbian relations at all) come to love each other, move in with each other and share their lives while having regular sexual intercourse, they are almost certainly doing something unlike anything *anybody* in ancient Israel did. The cultural contexts inevitably generate different practices.[4]

This does not mean, of course, that these Leviticus texts (or any of the other biblical texts that allude to homosexual behavior) have nothing to contribute to the pastoral care and guidance of the Henderson family in the congregational context. Surely they do. It does mean, however, that the connections between these texts and the contemporary context cannot be made simply or purely analogically. As Placher goes on to say, "So—when the Bible condemns some activities that were being done in ancient Israel, should we assume that it also condemns . . . differently contextualized activities today? I'm not sure I know the answer to that question—my point is simply that it is a complicated question."[5]

Placher is correct; the question is complicated, and what makes it so is that a pastoral, congregational awareness of the concrete circumstances of peoples' lives causes any easy analogy to break down. When we think clearly and analogically, claims Susan Thistlethwaite, we probe the unknown by inquiring about the known. "We learn something new both from the similarity and from the dissimilarity. The tension of the dissimilarity probes us to ask again."[6]

Thus, no matter what we think we are doing when we interpret the Bible, a congregationally based process of biblical interpretation inevitably favors poetry over precision. It is this "tension of dissimilarity" that Thistlethwaite names that tilts the hermeneutical balance toward poetry and imagination. Since we cannot forge an exact match between any circumstance in the Bible and any circumstance today, we must bring them together through the more chancy practice of metaphor and persuasion. However much we would like to develop a predictable and stable formula for interpreting scripture, the truth is that biblical texts connect to congregational life not by ineluctable logic but rather by what seems to the faithful imagination to be an apt fit. As I have stated elsewhere in regard to preaching,

> [W]hen preachers say, "Aren't we just like the Pharisees today?" or when they treat Abraham and Sarah as if they were neighbors down the street, they are not really forging an exact analogy, or moving with precision between discrete historical eras. Rather they are depending upon the creative capacity of the hearer to enter imaginatively into the world of a character in a story. When the preacher joins the text about the meat controversy at Corinth to, let us say, a local dispute about religion in the public schools, this connection is not obvious or mechanical; it results from the preacher's exercise of imagination, and its aptness must be judged on grounds other than strict, mechanical logic.[7]

An astonishing thing about this looser, more poetic style of congregational biblical interpretation is that it operates, I would maintain, even when people believe themselves to be working more methodically and logically, or strive to do so for doctrinal reasons. "Duncan Henderson," we are told by the *Wall Street Journal,* "always believed he could find answers in the Bible." What this probably means is that Duncan Henderson, if asked to articulate his understanding of the way the Bible teaches, would have outlined an analogical approach: pose the question, find the corresponding spot in the Bible, draw out the answer. But, in the press of struggling with his son, a more authentic picture of his biblical hermeneutics develops. When the church employed scripture (among other forces) to bar Paul from ordination, the fit between scripture and circumstance did not seem apt to Duncan.

Duncan is but one person, of course, and his sense of the lack of scriptural aptness certainly did not reflect the consensus of the presbytery or the

larger Presbyterian Church. Sorting out the various levels—personal, congregational, ecclesial—and adjudicating the potential conflicts of interpretation is important business, but the basic point remains: At every level
scriptural warrants for theological and ethical positions are based on an
imaginative and poetic sense of fit between scripture and context.

This claim inevitably raises the question of the role of experience in biblical interpretation, an issue too complex for a detailed analysis here. However, the basic issue can be named at least. In an important article on the
Bible and human sexuality, Christopher R. Seitz maintains, "In the sexuality
debate or any other like it, we are taught by Scripture that appeals to states
of nature or human experience as revelatory for the purposes of God in
Christ demonstrate nothing, in spite of their extraordinary hold at present."[8]

Seitz issues an important warning. Hearing a story like that of the Hendersons may move us to tears, inspire us, deepen our awareness of God's
presence, and so on; but no matter how much we are affected, the fact remains that the Henderson's story stands on different theological ground
than scripture. Human experience is not revelatory or authoritative in the
sense held by scripture.

Once we have heeded this warning, though, we must also recognize that
a sharp distinction between scripture and experience cannot be logically
maintained: Experience is in the Bible, the Bible has already shaped our experience, and so forth. Moreover, and more to the point, the Bible is not a
repository of religious ideas, but a force-field that exerts a shaping influence
over the life of Christian congregations and their members. In congregational context, what makes a biblical interpretation "right" or "valid" is not
only that it possesses integrity of a historical and grammatical sort, but also
that it edifies the church, that it summons faithful experience, that it forms
fidelity to the mission of Jesus Christ. Sandra M. Schneiders has called this
criterion for valid scriptural interpretation "fruitfulness." Any interpretation of the Bible that makes no difference in the experience of the faith
community—no matter how correct it may be on other grounds—must be
questioned.[9]

When Duncan Henderson, in the depth of his anguish, found meaning
in a passage from James, he was demonstrating this interaction between
scripture and experience. A text from James that has nothing to do with homosexuality per se engaged the grieving experience of the father of a homosexual man with AIDS to create the possibility of a more redemptive and
Christlike response to this human tragedy. No one could have predicted
that part of a biblical understanding of homosexuality would come from
this text or in this way, but the text proved salvifically useful, and this is one
measure of validity in interpretation.

*Finally, in congregation life, the "oracular" model of scripture is replaced by a
conversational one.* Of course, the picture of Christian communities facing

dilemmas and going to scripture for wisdom and guidance offers both desirability and truth. But when this is oversimplified, when scripture is depicted as an oracle consulted and heeded, the picture is distorted.

A Christian congregation is actually like a complex, ongoing, and multi-faceted conversation. A congregation, in John McClure's delightful phrase, is "talking itself into becoming a Christian community."[10] Preaching, teaching, praying, deliberating, praising, and sharing life around the coffeepot are all forms of the continuing congregational conversation, and scripture is a voice in the colloquy. Scripture is an important, authoritative, and normative voice—a "loud" voice, so to speak—but in congregational context it exerts its power conversationally and not unilaterally.

Part of what this means is that congregations employ a broad and sophisticated hermeneutic that relates the whole and the part—the whole of congregational life to the part of a given text of scripture. This bears similarity to canonical approaches to biblical interpretation in which the textual part is often seen as part of a larger whole as manifested by the canon. Thus a text can be heard in its own right, as a voice in the chorus, but its force is modified (and sometimes mitigated) by the overarching canonical harmonies.

In congregations, however, the textual part is related not just to the canonical whole, but to the whole of congregational life. Thus, many African American congregations are able to maintain an extraordinarily high view of biblical inspiration while relegating many individual texts (e.g., the slaveholding passages) to positions of insignificance. These texts simply exert little or no power when placed in the larger whole of the congregational life and faith. They are in the conversation, but the conversation is flowing in other ways, and these texts, while not banished, simply do not have much to say.

More specifically to our concern, when the Jennings Presbyterians listen to the Bible regarding sexuality (whether through sermons, church school lessons, private study, or reports from the denomination) those texts are entered into conversation with everything else that the people of Jennings know about the Christian life and about the Hendersons. It may be that Duncan's heartsick response to the refusal of the church to allow Paul to be ordained ("Paul was never a problem. . . . Still, they wouldn't have anything to do with him.") is just the cry of a wounded father, but it may also be the consensus view of the congregation at Jennings, a congregation that receives the more negative biblical and theological words about homosexuality in the context of all that they know about Paul Henderson and his Christian commitment. Of course, this can be merely sentiment, but it can also be baptismal discernment. What congregations observe, know, discern, feel, and experience inevitably enters into the dialogue with scripture. That is the way it is; that is the way it should be.

Manna for the Journey

"Duncan Henderson grew up on a wheat farm, walked two miles to school every day and always believed he could find answers in the Bible." In the context of the Presbyterian Church of Jennings, Missouri, in the preaching in the sanctuary and the laughter in the churchyard, in the hymns and in the prayers and in the reading of the lessons, in the touch of a hand at hospital bedside and in the words of comfort at the communion table, in the phone calls from members and in the printed reports of denominational deliberations—in every place in that congregation's life where the voice of scripture is invited to join the confusing welter of conversation about the even more entangled business of being Christian in the midst of the human condition—it is the conviction of the church that the spirit of God speaks. Perhaps Duncan will not hear the clear answers he seeks—maybe none of us will—but at least there will be a word of nourishment and hope, manna to go on one more day in faith. And that is enough.

NOTES

1. Judith Valente, "Love Story: How a Father and Son Discovered Each Other in the Shadow of AIDS," *The Wall Street Journal* (March 16, 1992): A1, A8. The descriptions and quotations of the Hendersons' story that follow are all taken from this article.
2. For examples of such criticisms of seminaries, see John H. Leith, "On Choosing a Seminary Professor," *The Presbyterian Outlook* 177, no. 8 (February 27, 1995): 6–7, 11; Jim Singleton, "Is It Time for a New Type of Seminary?" *The Presbyterian Outlook* 177, no. 28 (July 24–31, 1995): 8–9; and Thomas C. Oden, *Requiem: A Lament in Three Movements* (Nashville: Abingdon Press, 1995), esp. 40–41.
3. Charles M. Wood, *The Formation of Christian Understanding: An Essay in Theological Hermeneutics* (Philadelphia: Westminster Press, 1981), 19.
4. William C. Placher, "Is the Bible True?" a paper of the Center of Theological Inquiry, Princeton, N.J., no date, 7.
5. Ibid.
6. Susan Brooks Thistlethwaite, "Every Two Minutes: Battered Women and Feminist Interpretation," in *Weaving the Visions: New Patterns in Feminist Spirituality*, ed. Judith Plaskow and Carol P. Christ (San Francisco: Harper & Row, 1989), 304. See also Thomas G. Long, "The Use of Scripture in Contemporary Preaching," *Interpretation* 44, no. 4 (1990):341–52.
7. Thomas G. Long, 347–48.
8. Christopher R. Seitz, "Human Sexuality: Viewed from the Bible's Understanding of the Human Condition," *Theology Today* 52, no. 2 (1995): 242.
9. Sandra M. Schneiders, *The Revelatory Text: Interpreting the New Testament as Sacred Scripture* (San Francisco: HarperCollins, 1991), 165.
10. John S. McClure, *The Roundtable Pulpit: Where Leadership and Preaching Meet* (Nashville: Abingdon Press, 1995), 50.

7

But Isn't "It" a Sin?

Mark McClain-Taylor

I will argue that "it" is not, that homosexual practice in itself, is not sinful. The severe ambiguities, which plague those who would use the scripture alone or the sciences alone (or both somehow together) to ground their judgments about homosexuality as "sin," show those negative judgments to have their origins somewhere else. Consequently, I argue that assessing the appropriateness of homosexual practice as such, while not ignoring scripture or the sciences, should be done more in relation to the pervasive (but often implicit), *theo-ethical construals* we hold of what God is doing in the world.

A "theo-ethical construal" is an orienting imaginative act wherein Christians fuse their interpretations of what God is doing in the world (hence, "theo-") with what they take to be "the good" that God is thought to be working (hence, "-ethical"). These construals will also be varied and conflicting, but when they are foregrounded, the discussion of whether homosexuality is a sin, takes a different turn. It is at this point, especially, that I argue that it is difficult to hold homosexuality as such to be a sin in the sense of contravening our pervasive theo-ethical construals.

An Argument "On Location"

As with all theologians, my argument is socially located. As critically formulated, however, it cannot be reduced simply to the dynamics of my complex location. Nevertheless, my position is influenced by my thirteen years of teaching in a Protestant seminary, a place of both struggle and support.

For a number of reasons, I have found myself listening to, and increasingly challenged and instructed by, Christian students who dared to let me know what their lives were like as gay/bisexual/lesbian persons in this place. In the course of learning with and from them, I have never been led to instruct them on how their homosexual orientation might be in itself wrong for them. In fact, my prima facie obligation has been to resist interpretations of their orientations as "sinful." A praxis of care, involving constant circling between reflection and advocacy, increasingly led to my rejection of notions that homosexual practice in itself is a sin. This chapter briefly summarizes the main lines of the argument supporting such a praxis of care.

In a sense, this chapter is written for students Bill and Jane[1], who one day risked letting me know how their breakups with their respective partners were so similar to those of heterosexuals. I write for Raul who shared with me, in a way that would rival many a heterosexual person's maturity in love, how he has worked out an ethic of faithfulness to his mate. I write for Ella, Fred, and Sara, all of whom have been disowned by parents to varying degrees after their "coming out." I write for Mary and Daniel, both of whom are in different homosexual relationships and both parenting children growing up with straight sexual orientations. I write for Sally and Robert, both of whom started their ministries with exciting college chaplaincies, only to find no acceptance or place to work because of their sexual orientations.

I write *for* them, not in the sense of replacing their speech or being some necessary advocate for them, but in the sense of writing toward that for which they dream and for which we might all dream together. In the future, perhaps, there will appear a volume from this institution's faculty that allows gay/bisexual/lesbian thinkers themselves to write from the vantage point of an "out" and articulate gay or lesbian identity. It is a testimony to the lack of safety in much theological dialogue today that such voices are not now present in this volume. In the meantime, we can dream and labor.

Maybe I write also for my straight colleagues and friends. Many within the administration of my employing institution, several faculty colleagues, many students, some of my closest straight friends and loves believe my advocacy as a straight male for gay and lesbian practice is an act of unfaithfulness to the Christian faith, a presently misguided viewpoint, or a puzzling anomaly. I write for them, too, not to convert them so much as to be better understood by them.

The Ambiguities of Scripture

I use the term "ambiguity" throughout this chapter in the general sense of a feature that creates vagueness, uncertainty, and lack of clarity, such that a definitive negative judgment against homosexual practice is not warrantable. I will say just enough, in this section, about three ambiguities that make problematic our uses of scripture for rendering homosexual practice sinful.

The Ambiguity of Biblical Exegesis

Biblical exegesis is the disciplined reading and study of biblical texts. Such exegesis may employ different types of historical-critical, literary-critical and socio-political methods of explanation. It is one of the jobs of a theological institution to equip its students with the languages and skills necessary for disciplined exegesis.

Ambiguity enters if we recall that theological and moral convictions about homosexuality and other issues are never *only* the result of exegetical rigor. Exegetical explanation is always shaped by broader and often tacit "understandings" held by exegetes.[2] We cannot assess a theological conviction or a moral practice only by exegesis. Theologians and ethicists do not live by exegesis alone.

This does not simply cast exegesis to the subjective whims of the exegete's preferences and particularities. It does, however, challenge exegetes to be conscious about the ways certain preferences and particularities are always at play amid exegetical procedures.

Years ago, David Kelsey, in his book *The Uses of Scripture in Recent Theology*, wrote of the importance of an "imaginative construal" in interpreting the Bible.[3] His point is still crucial to recall: biblical readings, especially those presented as authoritative, usually depend upon imaginative, often holistic judgments that are not a mere product of exegetical work itself. Kelsey's point has been ably reinforced by hermeneutical studies, whether we recall Bultmann's familiar dictum about there being no "presuppositionless exegesis," or studies in the sociology of knowledge, or literary criticism—each testifying to the constant circling movement between exegeted texts and the worlds of "flesh-and-blood" exegetes.[4]

The pervasive presence of such imaginative construals in exegesis makes moral and theological conclusions susceptible to the exegete's visionary background and tacit understandings. Exegetical conclusions are especially ambiguous, and thus to be suspected, if there is no acknowledgement by exegetes of their tacit presuppositions, social location, and preunderstandings. Even with such an acknowledgment, "solid exegesis" can often yield remarkably divergent conclusions.

The Ambiguity of Particular Scripture Texts about Homosexuality

The ambiguity here is not simply that the Bible says both a yes and a no to homosexual practice. There is no clear yes, that I know of, and any such claims that scripture affirms what we know today as homosexual orientation would be anachronistic and strained at best. Here, I am mainly concerned with ambiguity in the texts often used to condemn homosexual practice.

Of the eight possible references for disapproval of homosexuality, only two (Lev. 18:22 and 20:13) clearly indicate and condemn homosexual relations, even to the point of demanding physical punishment and death. The other six passages (Genesis 19, Rom. 1:18–32, 1 Cor. 6:9, 1 Tim. 1:10, and Rev. 21:8 and 22:15), which are frequently used to ground the "sinfulness" of homosexuality, are questionable as even having to do with our topic. This is signaled by the fact that the Greek terms in those texts, which recently have been interpreted as meaning "homosexual," have been translated variously in the history of the Bible, for example, as effeminate, as abusers, as masturbators, as sexual perverts.[5] Many other exegetes have pointed out that these passages condemn not so much homosexuality as other harmful practices such as inhospitality, male temple prostitution, and certain inappropriate *kinds* of homoerotic behavior. Such ambiguities keep these texts from functioning as clear scriptural prohibitions of homosexual practice.

As to the Leviticus passages that remain allegedly relevant to contemporary homosexual practice, much depends on how exegetes place the Leviticus code and its strictures within the historical and literary contexts of the Hebrew Bible. For some, the Leviticus strictures lose their compelling force for us today because they were part of the stabilizing strategy of an elite Persian-backed priesthood seeking to shore up their class privilege and patriarchal dominance over other Jewish groups and ethnicities.[6] For others, our nearly unanimous refusal as twentieth-century Christians to enact the Levitical penalty of death for homosexuals and adulterers already sanctions a tradition of resisting the Leviticus code as "definitive" for today's Christian life. These are examples of the issues that render these scriptural texts ambiguous for grounding a clear negative judgment of homosexual practice.

The Ambiguity of Scriptural Authority

The ambiguity here is that scriptural authority has never been a matter of simply obeying the written word, the text, by itself. A positive place has often been given to other dynamics in interaction with the written word. For Calvin, it was Spirit at work in the believer that joined with Word for the experience of authority.[7] For others, some mode of communal consensus or respect for subsequent Christian traditions of interpretation was required for biblical authority. When scriptural authority is understood in these interactive ways, involving text *with* spirit, *with* community, or *with* tradition, then the words of the text and the textual codes, while remaining relevant, are not themselves the primary locus of authority.

In fact, it is part of the ambiguity of scriptural authority that portions of the word are downplayed or resisted, even while the scriptures are revered as authoritative for thought and practice. Scholar Renita Weems recalls, as one example, the Christian slave woman who had a love of the Bible and of preaching from it, but who also resisted crucial components in it, especially those where Paul seemed to affirm that slaves be obedient to their masters. "I promised my maker," she said, "that if I ever learned to read and if freedom ever came, I would not read that part of the Bible."[8]

That strategies of resistance to the Bible can be held alongside respect for its authority is an ambiguity leaving open the door for affirming something like homosexuality even in the face of seeming prohibitions in the biblical text. This accounts for the logic in what one respected, Reformed colleague of mine once said about the Bible and homosexuality: "I don't see why we can't confess that the Good Book was just wrong on this one."

The Ambiguities of the Sciences

I use the term "sciences" to refer to disciplined studies of homosexuality that emerge from outside the classical sources of Christian theology. Christians seeking to sustain their negative judgments about homosexual practice often employ material from these sources in order to show that the practice is "against nature."[9] Similarly, Thomas Aquinas long ago had argued that homosexuality was a vice against nature and so a violation of the will of God, the will of the One who has created nature.[10]

The argument that homosexuality is a sin because it is unnatural has, therefore, a long tradition. Today, this argument ranges from rough-and-ready dismissals of homosexuality as a disgusting "perversion" of nature, to theologians and other scholars citing studies to warrant claims that homosexual practice is deleterious to oneself or to human life and, therefore, a violation of creation and Creator—hence, a sin.

Severe ambiguity attaches to each type of these "natural law" arguments. Before looking at the ambiguities that I see in three major modes of these, note first an ambiguity pertaining to all science.

Ambiguity Attaching
to Scientific Inquiry Generally

Scientific method, whether in the natural or social sciences, does not possess a rigor or discipline that is completely independent of types of personal or communal bias. Disciplined methods bring new perspectives and materials and, thus, can challenge our first impressions, our tacit assumptions, and our initial value judgments.

Challenged and critically assessed though they may be, these assumptions and the passion that often goes with them usually remain in some implicit or explicit relation with disciplined science. Paul Ricoeur thus speaks of the dialectical relations between scientific methods and inquirers' guesses (and existential meanings).[11] Only a naive empiricism presumes to produce "objective" knowledge divorced from the scientists' "fore-conception" (Heidegger), or from "pre-judgments" (H. G. Gadamer).[12] Disciplined rigor is often fueled by tacit passions that make even mathematical exactness (as in Einstein) a very "personal knowledge" (M. Polanyi).[13] The results of scientific work, then, give not just "hard data," but ways of interpreting within "paradigms" that are supported or sometimes altered by communities of flesh-and-blood inquirers.[14]

All this is not to discount the value of scientific rigor and data. As theologians conducting inquiry in today's world, we ignore them to our peril. We often do need to remind ourselves, however, that scientists are human beings with their own prejudgments. Their results need to be examined in relation to their social locations, personal legacies, and commitments. Just as much as biblical exegetes, scientists depend upon certain "imaginative construals." Scientific data, especially about homosexuality (both pro and con), have to be examined not only against other contravening evidence, but also with consciousness about the different communal or personal paradigms that sustain and make plausible scientists' data. Amid scientific data, then, are a host of interpretive complexities that render negative *and* positive judgments about homosexuality difficult and ambiguous.

Ambiguities in Arguments from "Natural" Processes

The form of argument here may strike some readers as humorous, but arguments that homosexuality is sinful because no analogous processes can be found in nature or the animal kingdom have quite seriously been put forward at ecclesial panels, as well as dorm discussions. "Natural" life, so it is argued, develops in accord with sexual *difference.* Homoerotic activity is a force moving against the natural creation process of mating across differences. The problematic ambiguities here are two.

First, the very use of such an argument is ambiguous as a guide for contemporary moral practice. What, after all, does turning to natural process and the animal kingdom prove? In itself, little. This is evidenced by the history of Christians attempting such moves. Usually, arguments from natural process or the animal creation have been used in several, often contradictory ways. One practice that Christians wished to disparage could be called "against nature," while another practice might be disparaged because it is all *too* natural, or "bestial." James Weinrich once observed adroitly, "When animals do something that we like, we call it 'natural.'" When they do something that we don't like, we call it 'animalistic.'"[15]

In a single night of more than one presbytery's debate, I have heard homosexual practice faulted for being both "against nature" and a descent to "the level of beasts." Given that to be a beast, an animal, is one way to be in accord with nature—a nature originating from and sustained by the Creator—a listener might understandably be confused. Perhaps there are ways to clarify the speakers' intentions and thus the listeners' confusion, but the basic point is that such arguments seem based less on an interest in being in harmony with God's creation and more on an attempt to disparage homosexual practice by whatever means is most convenient.

This ambiguity is further complicated by a second issue. No evidence from natural process and/or the animal kingdom shows homosexual analogues to be completely absent. True, mating across sexual differences remains a powerful principle of life, but it is not an exclusive one. "Chaos theorists" remind us that life is more complex than growth through friction of binary terms.[16] Hence, in the animal kingdom itself, while heterosexual practice may remain the basic dynamism for reproduction of species, we do find possible analogues to human homoerotic behavior among a long list of species, including mice and marten, rams and stallions, from insect worlds to primates, from dolphins to gulls.[17] But again, what does this show? Little, beyond the fact that what is defined as natural is quite malleable indeed. There is hardly sufficient material here for forging widespread moral condemnation of homosexuality as "unnatural."

Ambiguities of Crosscultural Data

It is also often argued that from a crosscultural perspective most cultures, if for no other reason than to continue the species, have decided to regard heterosexual practice positively and to render negative judgment on same-sex eroticism.

In the first place, we again need to resist the automatic assumption that moral reasoning should take its cues about what is "good" from whatever is the most crossculturally pervasive practice. Male dominance, as anthropologist Peggy Sanday has shown, is overwhelmingly pervasive to human cultures, if not universal.[18] That does not mean, however, that this dominance warrants ratification as a desirable state of affairs. Even assuming that what is interculturally prevalent might be suggestive of a wisdom worked out by humankind over centuries of evolution, we note some persisting ambiguities that would question this principle in the case of homosexual or homoerotic activity.

A first general ambiguity is that crosscultural studies do not yield a uniform viewpoint. As argued by Wainwright Churchill, "There is little agreement among diverse cultures as to what is acceptable sexual behavior."[19] Second, while one can indeed enumerate many cultures that penalize homoerotic behavior, one can also name as many as forty-nine in which homosexual activities of one sort or another are considered normal and socially acceptable for certain members of the community. Almost every continent is represented in the list of cultures that feature a positive regard for homosexual practice: the Aranda, Aymara, Azande, Chamorro, Chukchee, Creek, Drow, Dahomeans, Easter Islanders, Hidatsa, Hopi, Lago, Madan, Menomini, Maskapi, Navajo, Palauans, Papago, Twana (females only), Witoto, Zuni, and others.[20]

Moreover, anthropologists have argued that some cultural approval of homosexual practice offers benefits that are lacking in more punitive cultures. The benefits include new ways to reinforce childcare, educate children, strengthen same-sex friendships and enrich religious and spiritual life.[21] While advocates for full acceptance of gay and lesbian practice use such literature to argue *for* that acceptance, I am citing the materials here only to establish the ambiguity that makes the crosscultural record unavailable for grounding negative judgments about homosexuality. In other words, there are simply too many cases of homosexual practices in other cultures, often as a sanctioned enrichment of kinship and family life, for one to argue convincingly that crosscultural data offers some universal collective wisdom that would rule out homosexuality as an intrinsic part of God's creation of diverse humanity.

Ambiguities of Pathological Studies

The studies I have in mind here are those that variously argue that homosexuals are "maladjusted." Often this claim is simply stated, emanating from personal feelings of disgust. When the claim is related to certain studies, three problems with those studies still remain, rendering them ambiguous.

First, such studies have been of gay/bisexual/lesbian persons who were already seeking psychiatric help, members of prison populations, or clients in mental health institutions. The sampling of the homosexual community has been insufficient, therefore, for grounding any negative judgments about the psychological health of gay/bisexual/lesbian persons in general. There are few, if any, studies of successful professionals or devoted parents who are also practicing homosexuals.

Second, none of these studies, to my knowledge, have combined wider sampling of homosexual populations with wide sampling of heterosexuals in order to provide a control group. Without such a control group, we have little way of knowing what perceived problems are due to homosexual practice, and what are due to other factors.

Third, any such studies of "maladjustment" need to take account of the added traumas borne by oppressed groups. Theories about maladjustment of homosexuals without a theorization of the special traumas created by a social matrix that ostracizes, silences and places stress on them, renders the talk about maladjustment problematic indeed. It easily can fault gay sufferers of discrimination for being sufferers. Without a theorization of homophobia[22] and its impacts on homosexuals, we will have little sense of what it means to adjust or to be maladjusted at all. Surely we will have little basis to argue that such maladjustment is evidence that homosexual practice itself is dangerous to the homosexual or to others.

Not only are these studies questionable in themselves, but subsequent studies have been undertaken that seek to implement the corrective controls. Because of these other studies, the American Psychological Association (APA) has taken homosexuality off the list of mental disorders. It is not a disorder, from the APA's perspective, for which professional counselors should seek "cures" or "changes" within a pathological framework. Whatever the nature of acute stress or dysfunction—abusive childhood, improper placement of infantile loves and drives, presence or absence of same-sex or opposite-sex parent, exposure to promiscuous behavior that is destructive—on nearly all these alleged indicators of traumas that might cause maladjustment, no evidence exists that homosexuals are, as such, more maladjusted than others.[23]

In sum, the uses of the sciences and scripture are, at best, ambiguous for providing grounds for a negative judgment on homosexual practice. For Christians, this need not make scripture and science irrelevant to their debates, but the ambiguities do drive us to some other resources. What might these be? As one response to that question, I close with a final plea for a *theo-ethical* hermeneutic of grace and sin.

A Plea for a Theo-ethical Hermeneutic

At first blush, my concluding plea may seem banal or simplistic. It may seem a meager contribution to the furious and complex debates. If taken seriously, however, I believe it adds an important dimension to debates about homosexuality's acceptability that I often do not see foregrounded.

The plea is that both those who accept and those who reject homosexual practice do so in relation to a clear articulation of what they interpret "the Christian thing" (G. K. Chesterton) to be, or the "heart of the Christian message and existence" to be about.[24] What is the good that Christian faith and living are about? What precisely is the good news that Christians are attracted to?

What I am pressing for here is something beyond a repeating of scriptural positions (however studious), beyond a recounting of traditional viewpoints (however distinguished), and beyond scientific citation (however clothed in expertise). I am looking for consciousness about "the imaginative construal" whereby Christians sense that their God has done, or is doing, something good in and for the world. What is that ideal, that gift, that new being?

This imaginative construal, theo-ethical in character, is almost always a powerful shaping force in all our readings of scripture, tradition *and* the sciences. We need to come to consciousness about what our theo-ethical construals are, and not just about what we determine scripture, tradition, or science to say. All three of these latter may be utilized in that construal, but the theo-ethical construal is itself not simply a composite of them. It is a creative, synthetic move, with its own character and set of debates. Moreover, this theo-ethical construal is essential for a determination of what the sinful is—what the "bad news" is, if you will.

Diverse theologians have emphasized that sin and evil have meaning and definition against the background of some understanding of the good. Rosemary Radford Ruether stressed that identifying sin and evil always implies operative ideals of a good self, a good human condition, a good world.[25] Karl Barth agreed. Joining Friedrich Schleiermacher on this point,

Barth wrote, "Sin is in fact a part of the Christian consciousness of grace no less than grace itself. . . ."[26] Or, more clearly still, Barth wrote in the *Church Dogmatics* that "only when we know Jesus Christ do we really know . . . what sin is, and what it means. . . ."[27] The first question of import here, then, is How do we construe the phrase "know Jesus Christ?"

Each of these theologians knew well that ultimately our understandings of sin will remain unclear without a presentation of our understandings of grace, of the good that is held to be revealed, created, sustained, empowered by God. Sin is fundamentally what contravenes that good, what moves contrary to that good One's presence, being, or character.

If one judges a practice or orientation like homosexuality to be sinful, one must then show how that practice violates or moves against the good or is somehow contrary to the event of grace.

Can you express your theo-ethical construal of the event of grace? I often find answering this question to be a continual personal challenge for seminary students, long-experienced pastors, and some seminary teachers. It is important to foreground clear statements of these theo-ethical orientations since they usually operate implicitly anyway.

Does the event of grace, for you, pivot around the notion of reconciliation? If so, what do you mean by that term and how would homosexual practice in itself, carried out by a believer or someone else, contravene such reconciliatory activity? Does mystical communion with God, or personal relationship with Jesus somehow sum up for you what the intrinsic good of being a Christian is all about? Fine. How precisely does homosexual practice then contravene, disrupt, or damage *that* good? Does liberation figure prominently at the heart of your construal of the good?[28] How does or does not a homosexual lifestyle disrupt that liberating activity of God and so warrant the label "sinful?"

This style of questioning is what I mean by a theo-ethical hermeneutic of grace and sin—an interpretation of human fault *in light of* a clear interpretation of what is God's gracious activity in the world.

As varied as these construals might be, I must confess that I have not yet encountered one that would be violated by my full acceptance of the homosexuality of practicing gay/bisexual/lesbian persons. Of course I *do* encounter Christians who hold that the scriptures clearly prohibit homosexuality or who imply that God's grace is simply the power to obey scripture. Both of those positions, however, are problematic: the first, because scripture (as we have noted) is so ambiguous on this question, and the second, because scripture is never an end in itself (even from a biblical point of view!) since it points to and witnesses to, God's being and presence in the world. It is precisely for this that our construals are needed.

We need, then, to foreground our visions of the Christian good. Plurality and ambiguity will no doubt touch this area of discussion too. In fact, it may be just as conflictual as our discussions of homosexuality. The advantage gained, however, is that we will be foregrounding a crucial dimension of our debates that often only lurks, unthematized and undiscussed, beneath the surface of our contestations about homosexuality. My suspicion is that within our different positions on the acceptability of homosexuality, there persist very different theo-ethical visions of what the Christian life is all about. Until we include discussion of those implicit but competing theological paradigms for our living, we may not even know what we are fighting about when debating homosexuality—in spite of our many references to scripture, tradition, or the sciences.

So start here. Who do you say Christ is, and what is God doing through Christ? How, then, does homosexual practice contravene that good, if, in fact, it does?

NOTES

1. All the names here have been changed to protect the innocent.
2. This is, in fact, acknowledged by the Reformed tradition, which stresses the importance of a confessional tradition that orients approaches to scripture. The mood of the church, as continually reformed by the spirit of Christ at work in the churches' actions in the world, instructs biblical readers. I am grateful to Princeton colleague, Prof. Daniel L. Migliore, for this reminder.
3. David H. Kelsey, *The Uses of Scripture in Recent Theology* (Philadelphia: Fortress Press, 1975), 167–70.
4. For a summary of these diverse viewpoints, see Fernando F. Segovia, " 'And They Began to Speak in Other Tongues' " *Reading from This Place: Social Location and Biblical Interpretation in the United States,* ed. Fernando F. Segovia and Mary Ann Tolbert (Minneapolis: Fortress Press, 1995), 1–32.
5. See John Boswell, *Christianity, Social Tolerance and Homosexuality: Gay People in Western Europe from the Beginning of the Christian Era to the 14th Century* (Chicago: University of Chicago Press, 1980), 335–53, 411–12.
6. Gary David Comstock, *Violence Against Lesbians and Gay Men* (New York: Columbia University Press, 1991), 122–32.
7. John Calvin, *Institutes of the Christian Religion* 1.7.4 (Philadelphia: Westminster Press, 1967).
8. Renita J. Weems, "Reading *Her* Way through the Struggle," *Stony the Road We Trod: African American Biblical Interpretation,* ed. Cain Hope (Minneapolis: Fortress Press, 1991), 61–62.
9. See, for example, *Unnatural Affections: The Impuritan Ethic of Homosexuality and the Modern Church* (Franklin, Tenn.: Legacy, 1991).
10. Warren J. Blumenfeld and Diane Raymond, *Looking at Gay and Lesbian Life* (Boston: Beacon Press, 1989), 199–200.
11. Paul Ricoeur, *Interpretation Theory: Discourse and the Surplus of Meaning* (Fort Worth: The Texas Christian University Press, 1976), 75–79.
12. Martin Heidegger, *Being and Time,* trans. J. Macquarrie and E. Robinson

(New York: Harper & Row, 1927/1962), 191–93; H.-G. Gadamer, *Truth and Method*, 2d rev. ed. (New York: Crossroad, 1989), 277–306.

13. Michael Polanyi, *Personal Knowledge: Toward a Postcritical Philosophy* (Chicago: University of Chicago Press, 1958), 323–24.

14. Thomas S. Kuhn, *The Structures of Scientific Revolutions*, 2d ed. (Chicago: University of Chicago Press, 1970).

15. James D. Weinrich, *Sexual Landscapes: Why We Are What We Are, Why We Love Whom We Love* (New York: Charles Scribner's Sons, 1987).

16. Danah Zohar, *The Quantum Self: Human Nature and Consciousness Defined by the New Physics* (New York: Quill/William Morrow & Co., 1990), 25.

17. Blumenfeld and Raymond, 94–99; B. L. Hunt and M. W. Hunt, "Female-Female Pairing in Western Gulls, *Larus occidentalis*," *Science* 196 (1977): 1466–67.

18. Peggy Reeves Sanday, *Female Power and Male Dominance: On the Origins of Sexual Inequality* (Cambridge: Cambridge University Press, 1981).

19. Wainwright Churchill, *Homosexual Behavior in Males: A Cross-Cultural and Cross-Species Investigation* (Englewood Cliffs, N.J.: Prentice Hall, 1967).

20. C. S. Ford and F. A. Beach, *Patterns of Sexual Behavior* (New York: Harper & Brothers, 1951). Check the recent evaluations of this classic study in Blumenfeld and Raymond, 99–100.

21. Walter L. Williams, *Spirit and the Flesh: Sexual Diversity in American Indian Culture* (Boston: Beacon Press, 1988).

22. For one glimpse into these dynamics, see Comstock, 25–30.

23. Bayer's study still is one of the most thorough discussions of these issues in the psychological profession. Ronald Bayer, *Homosexuality and American Psychiatry: The Politics of Diagnosis* (Princeton: Princeton University Press, 1987).

24. See David H. Kelsey, *To Understand God Truly: What's Theological about a Theological School* (Louisville, Ky.: Westminster John Knox Press, 1992), 32–33, 109–10, 186–87.

25. Rosemary Radford Ruether, *Sexism and the God-Talk: Toward a Feminist Theology* (Boston: Beacon Press, 1983), 93–94.

26. Karl Barth, *The Theology of Friedrich Schleiermacher: Lectures at Gottingen, Winter Semester of 1923/24*, ed. Dietrich Ritschl, trans. Geoffrey W. Bromiley (Grand Rapids: Wm. B. Eerdmanns Publishing Co., 1982), 196. Cf. F.D.F.Schleiermacher, *The Christian Faith* (Philadelphia: Fortress Press, 1976), 371–73.

27. Karl Barth, *Church Dogmatics* 4.1 (Edinburgh: T&T Clark, 1956), 389. Thanks again to Prof. Migliore for this notation.

28. Elsewhere I have offered my theo-ethical construal of the Christ event, using as my key phrase, "reconciliatory emancipation." I have also discussed why I do not see homosexual practice to violate such an ideal. See Mark Taylor, *Remembering Esperanza: A Cultural-Political Theology for North American Praxis* (New York: Orbis Books, 1990), 175–89, 115–22, 219–25.

8

Speaking the Text and Preaching the Gospel

Charles L. Bartow

The text I wish to grapple with in this chapter is Rom. 1:18–32. The portion of that text given homiletical treatment is Rom. 1:26–27, Paul's statement regarding homosexual practice. The approach used to determine how to speak the text and preach the gospel in the light of it is confessional/biblical practical theology. A confessional/biblical practical theology starts by defining the preacher's task in terms of the confessional standards of his or her denomination. For our immediate purposes, then, we turn to the confessional standards of the Presbyterian Church (U.S.A.).

The Minister as Servant of the Word

The proclamation of the gospel always begins with the public reading of the scriptures upon which that proclamation is based. This is so because, as *The Confession of 1967* puts it:

> God's word is spoken to his church today where the Scriptures are faithfully preached and attentively read in dependence on the illumination of the Holy Spirit and with readiness to receive their truth and direction.[1]

Preachers do not have license to speak from the pulpit what they or their congregants want to hear. Instead they are obligated by the office to which they have aspired and been called[2] and by their ordination vows[3] to preach that truth, which belongs to Christ as he is attested in scripture.[4] Thus, the authority of preachers rests not in their persons, nor in their experiences, nor in their rhetorical or elocutionary abilities, nor in their credibility among their contemporaries, but in their faithful witness to that to which the scriptures themselves bear witness.[5] Clearly, this does not mean that in their attempts to follow faithfully the witness of the scriptural evangelists and apostles as they follow Christ, preachers cannot err. Preachers surely can err, not only individually but en masse, just as church councils can err.[6]

But their errors are to be discerned in the light of Holy Scripture—not by means contrary to it. Questions of obscurity or apparent contradiction in the scriptural witness likewise are to be clarified by the further elucidation of scripture.[7] Furthermore, the scriptures are to be read critically—that is, according to the rule of Christ and with due consideration given to their socio-cultural contexts. The aim of critical exegesis, exposition, and interpretation is, of course, the faithful hearing of and obedience to God's Word. The aim of such exegesis, exposition and interpretation is not to silence that Word or to compromise its authority.[8]

God alone—in Christ, by the power of the Holy Spirit *and with the words of scripture*—reigns supreme in the affairs of the church and the world. As stated in the Theological Declaration of Barmen: "Jesus Christ, as he is attested for us in Holy Scripture, is the one Word of God which we have to hear and which we have to trust and obey in life and in death."[9] The scriptures thus are not ours to do with as we desire. Quite to the contrary, they are the means by which God, in sovereign freedom, lays claim to human life in all its dimensions so that humanity may realize its chief end, which is "to glorify God, and to enjoy him forever."[10] So "the freedom of the glory of the children of God" (Rom. 8:21) is not their emancipation from God so that they may imagine for themselves and undertake any way of life agreeable to them. It is, instead, freedom at last to be and to do what is pleasing to God. It is not a triumph of the self, but a triumph *over* self. It is not the opportunity to get what one wants, but the power to set all wants aside wherever they may be in conflict with humanity's "chief end." An authoritative word from the pulpit, consequently, is marked not by human vaunt but by humility. It is offered in faithful deference to him who speaks "as one having authority" (Matt. 7:29) through the witness of evangelists and apostles whose words—often lacking credibility among those who first heard them—have been received in the church by inspiration of the Holy Spirit, as sacred scripture, the word of God written.[11] Once again *The Confession of 1967* speaks clearly to this issue and so is quoted at length.

> The one sufficient revelation of God is Jesus Christ, the Word of God incarnate, to whom the Holy Spirit bears unique and authoritative witness through the Holy Scriptures, which are received and obeyed as the word of God written. The Scriptures are not a witness among others, but the witness without parallel. . . .
>
> The Bible is to be interpreted in the light of its witness to God's work of reconciliation in Christ. The Scriptures, given under the guidance of the Holy Spirit, are nevertheless the words of men, conditioned by the language, thought forms, and literary fashions of the places and times at which they were written. They reflect views of life, history, and the cosmos which were then current. The church, therefore, has an obligation to approach the Scriptures

with literary and historical understanding. *As God has spoken his word in diverse cultural situations, the church is confident that he will continue to speak through the Scriptures in a changing world and in every form of human culture.*[12]

As preachers who would serve the Word and not seek to master it, we address these vexing questions: How do we speak Rom. 1:18–32 from the pulpit in our Lord's Day worship? And how do we preach the gospel, keeping in view particularly the apostolic witness given in Rom. 1:26–27? The answers to these questions cannot be sought apart from a careful exposition of the text.

Exposition of Rom. 1:18–32
(with particular attention to vv. 26–27)

An exhaustive, technical, verse-by-verse exegesis and exposition of Rom. 1:18–32 on the basis of the Greek text, sensitive to the history of interpretation of the passage, and fully informed by reference to the literature of Hellenistic Judaism and stoic philosophy (which Paul in all likelihood drew upon or alluded to at the time of his writing Romans), clearly cannot be undertaken in this chapter. Nevertheless, an attempt will be made to avoid what Ernst Käsemann called "global judgments" and the rush to premature "practical application."[13] Following the advice of Howard Tillman Kuist, Rom. 1:18–32 will be given structural-analytic attention. Interpretative judgments will follow as the move is made to consider how to read the text from the pulpit and how to preach the gospel in light of the text's witness. Said Kuist, "Since any given whole is greater than its parts and cannot function without them, it follows that structural attention should precede interpretative attention. Analysis should always precede synthesis. 'Image the whole,' said Browning, 'then execute the parts.'"[14] It also has been noted that Paul's rhetorical moves in Romans—particularly his patterns of arrangement and compositional style—always serve a material purpose.[15] Form and content thus inform one another, and structural analysis yields theological insight. These procedures of structural analysis do not guarantee a totally objective, and thus utterly unquestionable, reading of the text. But they do allow for a fair reading of it, a reading that gives the text its head, so to speak, and allows it some measure of "over-againstness" (if not full autonomy) in relation to its reader. The procedures also allow for responsible critique.

Romans 1:18–32 follows upon Paul's statement of his theme recapitulating "the whole doctrinal section, which covers eleven chapters in the letter."[16] Paul's theme is the gospel, which he defines as "the power of God for salvation to everyone who has faith, to the Jew first and also to the Greek. For in it the righteousness of God is revealed through faith for faith;

as it is written, 'The one who is righteous will live by faith'" (vv. 16–17).[17] Verses 18–32 are linked to Paul's statement of his theme by the preposition "for." What follows, then, points to the need for salvation[18] and, in part, elucidates the meaning of the righteousness of God.[19] Salvation is needed in order that human beings might stand before God as justified sinners[20] and so be delivered from a sentence of death in the final judgment.[21] This salvation is not a passive state. In fact, the case is quite the opposite: "Standing in salvation is both here and everywhere standing in obedience, that is, in the presence and under the power of Christ."[22] As for the righteousness of God, as Käsemann says:

> It speaks of the God who brings back the fallen world into the sphere of his legitimate claim . . . , whether in promise or demand, in new creation or forgiveness, or in making possible our service, and . . . who sets us in the state of confident hope and . . . constant earthly change. . . . we may summarize the whole message of the epistle in the brief and paradoxical statement that the Son of God is as our [Lord] the one eschatological gift of God to us and that herein is revealed simultaneously both God's claim on us and also our salvation.[23]

The need for salvation is evidenced in fallen humanity's rejection of God's claim. Verses 18–32, consequently, must be understood as a discourse revealing God's eschatological judgment in and through the conduct of a disaffected, disobedient, and idolatrous humanity, a humanity that, in foolish pride, considers itself out from under God's jurisdiction and the saving Lordship of Christ. In a word, vv. 18–32 give us Paul's anthropology of the fall.[24] It is an anthropology discussed with particular reference to the pagan-gentile world of Paul's own time. Yet "thinking in mythico-historical categories, [Paul] casts forth a blanket condemnation of humankind."[25] He includes everyone—Jew and Greek, the erudite and the untutored, the civilized and the barbarian of all times and places. No one escapes God's wrath. The wrath of God is God's uprightness,[26] God's righteousness or justice, manifest in the life of fallen humanity. It is not opposed to the power of salvation, but is, in fact, part and parcel of the exercise of that power in a world run amok. Apart from the gospel, humanity cannot even come to understand its true plight.[27] It is the gospel that shows us both our need of salvation and God's provision for it through the justification of the ungodly in Jesus Christ. God's righteousness (uprightness and justice) is thus vindicated. As Richard Hays has indicated, Paul's allusion to Habakkuk is no mere rhetorical flourish. It has material significance for his argument. It raises the spector of theodicy, the gnawing question of how the justice of God can be made known in a world of flagrant injustice.[28] Hear the prophet:

O Lord, how long shall I cry for help,
   and you will not listen?
Or cry to you "Violence!"
   and you will not save?
Your eyes are too pure to behold evil,
   and you cannot look on wrongdoing;
Why do you look on the treacherous,
   and are silent when the wicked swallow
      those more righteous than they?
                                                        (Hab. 1:2, 13)

Paul's answer to Habakkuk's anguished cry is given in Rom. 1:18–32, Paul's discourse on the wrath of God.

The discourse begins and ends with what should be self-evident. God's "eternal power and divine nature" (v. 20) have been disclosed to human beings *by God* "through the things he has made" (v. 20). Humanity "knew God" (v. 21) but "did not honor him as God or give thanks to him" (v. 21). Likewise in v. 32, we read that human beings "know God's decree, that those who practice such [evil deeds as follow upon idolatry] deserve to die—yet they not only do them but even applaud others who practice them."[29] Said Calvin:

> It is the height of evil when [sinners are] so completely void of shame that [they are] not only pleased with [their] own vices, . . . but also [encourage] them in others by [their] consent and approval. . . . Paul, it seems, meant to condemn here something more grievous and wicked than the mere perpetration of vice. I do not know what this may be, if we do not mean that which is the height of wickedness—when wretched [human beings], casting away all shame, undertake the patronage of vice rather than the righteousness of God.[30]

Paul's discourse on the wrath of God is bracketed by assertions regarding the human culpability that warrants God's wrath. This anthropology of the fall and of idolatry, which is not aimed at any one person or group in particular, but instead includes all human beings of all times and places, provides the context for the action of God that vindicates divine righteousness. It is this vindicating action of God that Paul calls God's wrath. And it is precisely the gospel, which is the power of God for salvation and which reveals the righteousness of God, that brings to light both God's wrath and the conditions that warrant it. If not for the good news of God's salvation and justice, human beings could never know their plight or the joy of deliverance from it. Note the rhetorical principle of return (or creative repetition, or echoing) that Paul uses to emphasize the accountability of humanity for its idolatry and ingratitude: Human beings have suppressed the truth concerning God that "they knew" (v. 21), and they have gone on to encourage such wickedness though "they know" (v. 32) full well that a sentence of death hangs over them.

Paul sustains this principle of creative repetition, return, or echoing throughout his discourse on God's wrath: "and *they exchanged* the glory of the immortal God for images" (v. 23); "*they exchanged* the truth about God for a lie" (v. 25). The phrases, "they exchanged" are followed by the assertions: "Therefore *God gave them up* in the lusts of their hearts to impurity" (v. 24); and "For this reason *God gave them up* to degrading passions" (v. 26). Finally, we read: "*And since they did not see fit to acknowledge God, God gave them up* to a debased mind and to things that should not be done" (v. 28). The phrase "and since they did not see fit to acknowledge God" echoes both "they knew" and "they exchanged." Thus it signals the climax of Paul's discourse on the wrath of God and the human condition of willful ignorance, idolatry, and ingratitude that occasions it. James D. G. Dunn points out the significance of this climactic moment. He writes that the signs of God's wrath are not manifest simply in the sexual irregularities discussed in vv. 26–27 but are manifest equally, and perhaps most significantly, in the general disorder of human society:

> The daily envy, deceit, whispering behind backs, heartlessness, ruthlessness, and so on, manifest human corruption quite as much, if not more than homosexual acts. Such homely, everyday vices which poison human relationships are as much a sign of [humanity's] loss of God as any sexual perversion.[31]

Nevertheless, the homosexual acts identified in vv. 26–27 *are* signs of God's wrath. Note that such acts—as well as envy, murder, strife, deceit, craftiness, gossip, slander, etc.—do not precede God's wrath and call it forth. Instead, such acts signify God's wrath in response to human ingratitude, idolatry, and self-deceit: "Claiming to be wise, they became fools" (v. 22). Homosexual behavior, boastfulness, rebelliousness, heartlessness, and the rest are the deeds God gave human beings up to as a result of their false pride—their desire, as Helmut Thielicke once expressed it, to be the "gods of God."[32] Human beings thought they could "be like God, knowing good and evil" (Gen. 3:5). They sought to become "autonomous moral agents" as is commonly said today. Instead they fell into moral confusion: "their senseless minds were darkened" (v. 21), and "God gave them up to a debased mind" (v. 28). Human beings were victimized by their own choices. They were enslaved to their own passions. They got hopelessly caught up in self-definition and self-imaging—chasing, grasping, trying to hold fast to the merest, vaguest, most shadowlike ghost of the good they would be without God.

For Paul, the moral being, the sexual orientation, the corporate character, and the personal identity are not things that human beings can responsibly forge for themselves, nor are they things ontogenetically determined. Such present-day proposals could not even have been entertained by the apostle or his contemporaries.[33] As a result, such proposals cannot legitimately be read into Paul's context in order to mitigate the force of his argument. For Paul, God's intention for humankind, apart from Christ, simply is lost on humanity because of its idolatry. Humanity's only hope, therefore, lies in the gospel that calls all people, through faith, to trust where they cannot see and to place all that they have, are, and can dare to become into the service of what God would have them be. Elsewhere in Romans, Paul states it this way: "you . . . must consider yourselves dead to sin and alive to God in Christ Jesus" (Rom. 6:11), out from under the things that belong to the wrath of God and fully engaged in those things that signify God's salvation. This is not perfectionism, for the saints of God are justified sinners, not sinless souls who need no justification. And this is no occasion for judgmentalism, homophobia, and self-righteousness. God alone is worthy to judge, and God judges in order to save, not to condemn. "Therefore you have no excuse, whoever you are, when you judge others," says Paul, "for in passing judgment on another you condemn yourself, because you, the judge, are doing the very same things" (Rom. 2:1). Rather, all human beings, homosexuals and heterosexuals together, are called to pursue life under the rule of Christ through continual confession and repentance. Neither is in a position to condemn or condone the other. God has judged humanity and *will judge* it, and the works that belong to God's wrath and to the righteousness of Christ, God has made known and will make known. Such is the word of the apostle.

The apostle's word, of course, is not regarded everywhere as reliable or relevant for the conduct of human affairs. Not only in the world at large but also in the church, some have argued that Paul's thoughts regarding homosexual practice in particular ought to be reconsidered in fresh ways that allow for the affirmation of homosexual behavior. If that cannot be done, perhaps his word on the subject simply should be abandoned, a proposal that Richard Hays has labeled "grave."[34] In Paul's own day, his stature as an apostle was put to the test. It seems he often had to defend his "reading" of the gospel.[35] The church at Rome (see Rom. 1:8–15) quite conceivably had its suspicions regarding Paul. In writing to that church, Paul apparently felt he had to explain himself, demonstrate his good intentions, and with some seeming discomfort, try to increase the readiness of the Romans to hear what he had to say.[36] He made it clear, nevertheless, that he "was not ashamed of the gospel" (v. 16), and whatever others might make of his witness to it, he was prepared to give that witness forthrightly. That he did.

John Boswell[37] and Robin Scroggs[38] have attempted to reread Rom. 1:26–27 in a way that mitigates its impact as a statement of total disapproval of all homosexual practice. Other scholars, notably Richard Hays, seem to have refuted their exegetical proposals.[39] It is beyond the scope of this essay to go into highly technical debates already thoroughly engaged by eminent biblical scholars. Nevertheless, the following conclusions may be drawn on the basis of those debates:

1. Romans 1:26–27 does not deal only with pagan, cultic homosexual activity.
2. Paul does not have in mind primarily—much less exclusively—pederastic homosexual activity.
3. Paul is not speaking about people who, by modern definition, are "naturally" heterosexual but who are indulging in what for them must be "unnatural" homosexual acts.
4. Paul is not buying into a concept of "natural" that means simply "true to the nature of things" according to the standard of an antiquated theory of biology, nor is he using the term "natural" to refer to merely conventional standards of behavior.
5. Paul *is* adopting a concept of situationally appropriate or fitting sexual activity, but the frame of reference he has in mind is God's created order and the new humanity in Jesus Christ, not simply a socio-cultural circumstance.
6. Paul's use of the phrase "contrary to nature" cannot be understood in a nonnormative sense of going beyond typical expectations, but, instead, must be understood as going beyond the bounds of God's created order and the claims of the gospel.
7. Though Paul's reference to homosexual practice is illustrative in character (the main theme of Rom. 1:18–32 is idolatry and ingratitude, as has been shown), it clearly is seen by the apostle as indicative of the wrath of God, and its connotation for him, his readers, and Hellenistic Judaism is profoundly negative.

One challenge to the traditional reading of Rom. 1:26–27 has not yet received much attention in print. That is the challenge presented by an application of J. Christiaan Beker's theory of "coherence" and "contingency." Says Beker:

> By "coherence" I mean the stable, constant element which expresses the convictional basis of Paul's proclamation of the gospel: he refers to it as "the truth of the gospel" (Gal. 2:5, 14), apostasy from which elicits an apocalyptic curse (Gal. 1:8, 9; see also Phil. 1:27; 2 Thess. 1:8, 2:12). By "contingency" I mean the variable element, that is, the variety and particularity of sociological, economic, and psychological situations which Paul faces in his churches and on the mission field. Thus through the interaction between coherence and contingency, the abiding Word of the gospel becomes a word on target, thereby fulfilling its function as gospel.[40]

There are those who would claim that Rom. 1:26–27 belongs to what is contingent in Paul's thought and not to what is coherent, "the stable constant element," the "truth of the gospel . . . , apostasy from which elicits an apocalyptic curse." The passage is illustrative of the wrath of God in terms appropriate to Paul's original readership, so the case might be argued. But there is no reason to see that illustrative material as enduringly valid and demonstrative of Paul's core teaching regarding the truth of the gospel. For reasons earlier alluded to, this argument cannot stand. It has been shown that Paul's rhetoric itself has material significance. It directs us to what matters theologically. And what matters theologically in Rom. 1:18–32 is precisely apocalyptic judgment (God's wrath) manifest in moral confusion, including homosexual conduct. If one were to say that the wrath of God in Paul's thought is not signalled by homosexual conduct, then by the same logic—and given the clear parallelisms of Paul's rhetoric—covetousness, malice, envy, murder, strife, deceit, faithlessness, heartlessness, and ruthlessness also could be excluded. Then none of us could find ourselves anywhere amid the ranks of fallen humanity or the ranks of the new creation in Christ, for the gospel would be powerless to disclose with any clarity at all either the wrath of God or the salvation of god. It is doubtful that many would care to take the options of the interpreter that far.

The word of the apostle regarding homosexual conduct appears unequivocal. And as Richard Hays has pointed out, there is no scriptural evidence or extrabiblical evidence in Christian literature up to the time of Constantine to refute it.[41] If one wishes to affirm homosexual practice, given the apostolic witness of Rom. 1:18–32 (especially vv. 26–27), one simply will have to take the grave step of rejecting the apostle's teaching. For those standing in the confessional tradition outlined above, and for preachers who have taken ordination vows consonant with that tradition, such a step, if taken, will be grave indeed.

Speaking the Text and Preaching the Gospel

In reading a passage of scripture from the pulpit, the minister is required to give the sense of it as clearly as possible. This is a matter of what W. J. Beeners has called "vocal exegesis" or intelligible phrasing and emphasis (grouping words into easily understood units of thought, telling one thing at a time, and stressing the appropriate word in each phrase so that ideational development is clear).[42] The minister also should follow the rhetorical or suasory movement of the passage so that its fulcrum (or crucial turning point)[43] and climax[44] are clear. In Rom. 1:18–32 the fulcrum and climax occur simultaneously with the words: "And since they did not see fit to acknowledge God, God gave them up to a debased mind" (v. 28). The moment of denouement[45] or resolution comes with v. 32: "They know God's decree, that those who practice such things deserve to die." The tensiveness[46] or creative conflict sustained throughout the passage is signaled by the parallelisms discussed earlier: "they knew God" (v. 21) and "they know God's decree" (v. 32) and the antitheses: "they exchanged" (vv. 23, 25, 26) and "God gave them up" (vv. 24, 26, 28). Thus the emotional content of the passage is evoked by its rhetorical structure, which at the same time provides the clue to its theological substance. The passage is full of subdued tension, clear intellectual struggle, and pastoral pathos.

This last thought gives us some idea of the persona[47] of the passage. The persona is the author as he presents himself speaking in the text (i.e., Paul). The preacher reading the text from the pulpit takes up the persona's point of view. How does Paul, as we experience him speaking in the text, position himself in relation to his subject matter and his audience? The context of the passage provides us with some clues. Paul, while "not ashamed of the gospel" (Rom. 1:16), clearly has some ambivalent feelings about how the Romans may receive him (Rom. 1:8–15). Further, his discourse on the wrath of God is not directed at particular persons or groups of persons in the church, but rather is aimed at humanity as a whole. Everyone is drawn into the picture of idolatrous and ungrateful humanity somewhere, including the apostle himself, no doubt. Also, in Rom. 2:1, Paul sounds his general warning about judging others: "Therefore you have no excuse, whoever you are, when you judge others; for in passing judgment on another you condemn yourself, because you, the judge, are doing the very same things." The attitude of the persona thus appears to be one of humility—Paul does not appear to be thinking of himself more highly than he ought—as well as careful pastoral urgency. The apostle does not attack the Romans or us. Instead he creates a place for us to stand to hear God speak today.[48] The word we hear is a disquieting word, to be sure. Hidden in it, though, is a promise; for the gospel that reveals God's righteousness and wrath is also God's power of salvation.

In preparing and delivering their sermons, particularly in focusing on Rom. 1:26–27, preachers will need to remember that. This text offers no justification for any vicious attack on homosexuals any more than it gives justification for attacking gossips, slanderers, God-haters, the insolent, haughty, boastful, foolish, faithless, heartless, and ruthless, for we are they. God has given us all up to "impurity," to "degrading passions," to a "debased mind," and "to things that should not be done." Nor is it appropriate, according to Paul's teaching, simply to tell people to give up these behaviors and to do better, for moral admonition has in it no power to accomplish what it insists upon.[49] Since God has given us up to "the lusts of [our] hearts," these lusts are our tyrants. We are enslaved to them— enslaved to sin, to use Paul's language. We are under sin's aegis, surrendered to its jurisdiction—except as Christ Jesus, by the power of his Holy Spirit, frees us from it and brings us into the sphere of his own obedience through faith. That is, we are to trust Christ and not ourselves. We are to

entrust ourselves to him. In Rom. 1:18–32—and in vv. 26–27 particularly—
Paul provides us not with an ethic but with a doctrine and a challenge: To
consider ourselves dead to sin—to homosexual practice, wickedness, evil,
covetousness, malice, envy, murder, strife, deceit, craftiness, gossip, slander, God-hating, insolence, haughtiness, boastfulness, evil intention, rebelliousness, foolishness, faithlessness, heartlessness, and ruthlessness. The
list sets the direction of Paul's thought clearly, but it is not comprehensive.
It could be extended, and we can imagine how! Yet the challenge is also
there to consider ourselves alive to God in Christ Jesus.

This is the context, "the ground of motivation for ethical action,"[50] into
which the ethical questions and the polity questions come flooding. Is it appropriate to ordain to the office of word and sacrament people who refuse
to repent of (to turn away from and disclaim the power of) those things
which do not belong to the obedience of Jesus Christ? Should the church
recognize, with ceremonies reminiscent of the order of worship for the sol-
emnization of marriage, the union of homosexual partners? What actions
might the church take—or fail to take—that might be construed as "applauding" (see Rom. 1:32) what people ought not to do? How does the
church avoid condoning—"applauding"—the judgmentalism that isolates
homosexual persons as somehow more offensive to God's righteousness
than heterosexuals who themselves engage in acts contrary to the obedience
of Christ? Such judgmentalism, according to Paul, also is a manifestation of
the wrath of God. It is pretentious, full of hubris. It is the "out-of-bounds"
aspiration of those who would be "like God." Paul caught the feel of our
dilemma: "Wretched man that I am!" he cried, "Who will rescue me from
this body of death" (Rom. 7:24)? Then in the same breath, he says: "Thanks
be to God through Jesus Christ our Lord!" Just so, through faith in Jesus
Christ who is Lord and whose sovereign sway sets us free from the tyranni-
cal powers to which God's wrath has delivered us up, do we move from idolatry to the worship of the one true God, and from ingratitude to praise.

> Now to God who is able to strengthen [us] according to . . . the
> proclamation of Jesus Christ . . . to bring about the obedience of
> faith . . . to the only wise God, through Jesus Christ, . . . be glory
> forever! Amen.
>
> (Rom. 16:25–27)

NOTES

1. *The Book of Confessions*, Presbyterian Church (U.S.A.), C 9.30.
2. The Second Helvetic Confession states: "The Preaching of the Word of God
   Is the Word of God." *The Book of Confessions*, Presbyterian Church (U.S.A.),
   C 5.004. For the full context of this assertion, however, see 5.001–5.007 and
   5.010–5.014. Also see 5.142–5.147 and, especially, 5.150–5.155.

3. *Book of Order*, Presbyterian Church (U.S.A.), G-14.0405.
4. *The Book of Confessions*, Presbyterian Church (U.S.A.), C 9.27ff.
5. Theories of authority vary, of course, between traditions, as David Bartlett makes clear in his article on the subject in *Concise Encyclopedia of Preaching*, ed. William H. Willimon and Richard Lischer (Louisville, Ky.: Westminster John Knox Press, 1995), 22–23. Apparently, not all traditions draw a sharp distinction between authority and ethos. Nevertheless, in the confessional tradition of the Presbyterian Church (U.S.A.), the distinction must be drawn. From the confessional perspective governing this essay, the influential work by Fred B. Craddock (*As One Without Authority* [Nashville: Abingdon Press, 1971]) presents a homiletic centered on a theory of ethos, not authority. Ethos has to do with how an audience views a rhetor's effort as compelling or authoritative *for it*. Thus, in traditional rhetorical theory, ethos is a mode of proof, a means of persuasion.
6. In *The Book of Confessions*, Presbyterian Church (U.S.A.), see C 5.167, C 6.175, C 9.03.
7. Ibid., see C 3.18, C 5.010, C 6.004–6.010, C 8.04, C 9.27–9.30.
8. For further elucidation of this point, see Leander E. Keck, *The Church Confident* (Nashville: Abingdon Press, 1993). See especially Keck's discussion of the "hermeneutics of alienation," at 59–65.
9. *The Book of Confessions*, Presbyterian Church (U.S.A.), C 8.11.
10. Ibid., C 7.001.
11. *The Book of Confessions*, Presbyterian Church (U.S.A.), C 3.18, C 5.001–5.003, C 6.002, C 9.27.
12. Ibid., C 9.27, C 9.29–9.30 (emphasis added).
13. Ernst Käsemann, *Commentary on Romans*, trans. and ed. Geoffrey W. Bromiley (Grand Rapids: Wm. B. Eerdmans Publishing Co., 1980), viii.
14. Howard Tillman Kuist, *These Words Upon Thy Heart* (Richmond: John Knox Press, 1947), 103.
15. See Richard B. Hays, "Relations Natural and Unnatural: A Response to John Boswell's Exegesis of Romans 1" *Journal of Religious Ethics*, 14, no. 1 (1986): 191–95; also, James D. G. Dunn, *Romans* in Word Biblical Commentary 38 (Dallas: Word, 1988), 67. Fitzmyer argues for considering Paul's rhetoric especially as the rhetoric of an orator and not a writer, so that Romans, when spoken, even more clearly evidences the link between rhetorical technique and theological content. See Joseph A. Fitzmyer, *Romans*, vol. 33, *Anchor Bible* (New York: Doubleday, 1993), 89–95.
16. Fitzmyer, *Romans*, 253.
17. Paul here is quoting Hab. 2:4.
18. Käsemann, 33–36.
19. Hays, 188–89.
20. As Käsemann puts it (p. 35): "As justification, the gospel always means deliverance from wrath, the justification of the ungodly, eschatological *creatio ex nihilo*. . . ."
21. C.E.B. Cranfield, *The Epistle to the Romans* I in International Critical Commentary (Edinburgh: T&T Clark, 1975), 134.
22. Käsemann, 29.

23. Ibid.
24. Dunn, 53; Käsemann, 190–91, 210. Also H. Darrell Lance, "The Bible and Homosexuality," *American Baptist Quarterly* 8 (1989): 147.
25. Hays, 189.
26. Fitzmyer, 253.
27. Käsemann, 34.
28. Hays, 188–89.
29. See Cranfield (p. 135) for an especially persuasive discussion of the greater culpability of those who applaud wrongdoing, as contrasted with the lesser, though profound, culpability of those who actually perpetrate wrongdoing.
30. Quoted in Cranfield, 135.
31. Dunn, 76.
32. Helmut Thielicke, *Between God and Satan*, trans. C. C. Barber (Grand Rapids: Wm. B. Eerdmans Publishing Co., 1958), 4.
33. Hays, 201.
34. Hays, 211.
35. A provocative thesis regarding Paul's self-presentation in defense of his apostolic authority is given by Richard F. Ward, *Paul and the Politics of Performance at Corinth: A Study of 2 Cor. 10–13* (Unpublished diss., Illinois: Northwestern University, 1987). See also Richard F. Ward, *Speaking from the Heart* (Nashville: Abingdon Press, 1992), 102–3.
36. Käsemann, 19–20.
37. John Boswell, *Christianity, Social Tolerance, and Homosexuality* (Chicago: University of Chicago Press, 1980), 107–17.
38. Scroggs, *The New Testament and Homosexuality* (Philadelphia: Fortress Press, 1983), 14–15, 109–118.
39. Hays, 184–215.
40. J. Christiaan Beker, "Recasting Pauline Theology: The Coherence-Contingency Scheme as Interpretive Model," in *Pauline Theology* vol. 1, ed. Jouette M. Bassler (Minneapolis: Fortress Press, 1991), 15.
41. Hayes, 202–4.
42. Charles L. Bartow, *Effective Speech Communication in Leading Worship* (Nashville: Abingdon Press, 1988), 32–54. Also G. Robert Jacks, *Getting the WORD Across* (Grand Rapids: Wm. B. Eerdmans Publishing Co., 1995), 75–100.
43. Charles J. Bartow, *The Preaching Moment: A Guide to Sermon Delivery*, 2d ed. (Dubuque: Kendall/Hunt, 1995), 21–31.
44. Ibid.
45. Ibid.
46. Bartow, *Effective Speech Communication in Leading Worship*, 20–22.
47. Judy E. Yordan, *Roles in Interpretation*, 3d ed. (Madison: Brown & Benchmark, 1993), 19–21.
48. Clark Pinnock, "The Inspiration and Interpretation of the Bible," *TSF Bulletin* 4, no. 1 (1980): 5.
49. A now-classic critique of moralistic preaching can be found in Leander E. Keck, *The Bible in the Pulpit* (Nashville: Abingdon Press, 1978), 100–105.
50. Hays, 207.

9
Homosexuality—What Then Shall We Preachers Say?

James F. Kay

As the issue of homosexuality began to surface in the mainline churches twenty years ago, Patrick Henry, a Presbyterian layperson and at the time a Swarthmore professor, noted that "there are articles aplenty on this subject." He added: "What we need is to hear more from the pulpit about it."[1] Henry's plea for more preaching on this disputed question recognizes the silence about sex that often shrouds the pulpit. As Jon M. Walton ventures to observe in a sermon, "The traditional answer to any nonmarital question about sex in the church is 'don't'; don't have sex, don't take pleasure in it, and please, don't talk about it."[2]

While we have not witnessed a flood tide of sermons on homosexuality, there has been a significant stream of them beginning in the 1970s. Among those who have dared to preach on the subject are William Sloane Coffin, Jr., and the late Channing E. Phillips. The former represents a reformist position; the latter takes a traditionalist view. In this chapter, I test how these preachers make their cases by applying three key criteria for doctrinal faithfulness. In the process, I hope to show that theological reflection on preaching, as well as preaching itself, can help us in answering the urgent question of what we shall say about homosexuality.

In order to keep focused and at the same time alert the reader to a sizable body of sermonic material, I supplement my examination of Coffin and Phillips by referring to a number of other preachers by way of notes. The preachers chosen are often, though not exclusively, working pastors. Most, but not all, are men; some, but not all, identify themselves as "straight," "lesbian," or "gay." ("Queer" as a self-identification has apparently not yet entered pulpit parlance.)

What these preachers each have in common are sermons that join those of Coffin and Phillips in taking seriously homosexuality as a disputed issue in the church. Since this has served as my chief criterion for sermon selection, I pass over sermons whose biblicist blinders prevent even the recognition of homosexuality as an issue.[3] Likewise, I pass over any number of sermons by self-identified lesbians or gays for whom, and in whose sympathetic congregations, homosexuality is no more a disputed topic than slavery is in the African-American church.[4] I have made sparing use of "coming out" sermons tapping them only as they touch on homosexuality, and not simply on "coming out."[5]

But what precisely is in dispute? I think the issue can be posed as follows: According to the Word of God or the gospel of Jesus Christ as attested in scripture, is the church to regard homosexuality as a gift of God's good creation or, contrariwise, as a sinful falling away from the Creator's intention for human creatures? In other words, does the phenomenon of homosexuality indicate a *variation* within God's created order (like left-handedness or red hair) or a *deviation* from the divine intention (like idolatry or adultery)? Is homosexuality an instance of created "difference" or, by contrast, of fallen "depravity"? As Jim Larson puts it, "Was I thus defective? An aberration or abomination? Or was I, like everybody else, an expression of God's wondrous diversity in creation?"[6]

For the Reformed tradition and, indeed, for much of Protestantism, the holy scriptures are taken as the unparalleled witness to the gospel of Jesus Christ through which the Holy Spirit illumines human hearts. They are normative for Christian teaching and preaching. Thus, in the words of the Second Helvetic Confession, "in controversies about religion or matters of faith" we are referred to "God himself, who proclaims by the Holy Scriptures what is true, what is false, what is to be followed, or what to be avoided."[7] But what is God proclaiming by the holy scriptures concerning homosexuality? No text of scripture explicitly approves of homosexual orientation or conduct as such, while Jesus, and the prophets before him, are silent on the subject. As both sides of the debate also recognize, passages that appear to condemn what we call homosexuality may not be doing so as such, or at all, or doing so only apart from the fullness of the gospel.[8] So what then shall we say? In seeking our answer, we now listen to what two preachers did say from the pulpit of the Riverside Church, New York City, in the early 1980s.

Controversy at Riverside: A Case Study

In the summer of 1981, William Sloane Coffin, Jr., former chaplain at Yale University and then Riverside's senior minister, preached soon after the U.S. House of Representatives voted "to bar the Legal Services Corporation from pressing cases where homosexuality is at issue." In his sermon, Coffin noted the widespread physical and psychological abuse of gays, their frequent exclusion from their families and churches, and the claim by some who speak for God "that gay men and women are not only different, but sinfully different." In Coffin's view, "We have no choice but to bring up the issue," which he characterized as "probably the most divisive since slavery split the Church."[9]

Coffin went on to argue from Acts 10 for the church to extend "unconditional acceptance" to homosexuals and to support "stable relationships" among gays. He recalled the story

> of Peter's struggle to abandon his own fixed certainties, to overcome his own repugnance. Three times he protests when in his trance he hears the Lord order him to rise and kill and eat birds and reptiles and pigs. Hardly surprising, when you remember that ever since he was a tot he has had it drilled into him: 'Every swarming thing that swarms upon the earth is an abomination; it shall not be eaten. Whatever goes on its belly, and whatever goes on all fours, or whatever has many feet, . . . they are an abomination.' That's Holy Writ, part of the holy Levitical Code (Lev. 11:42ff.), the Word of God as Jews understood it. And now God suddenly is telling Peter just the opposite: 'Kill and eat. . . . What God has cleansed, you must not call common.' Moreover, all his life Peter has been instructed not to associate with Gentiles. Nevertheless, when the three men arrive he accompanies them to Cornelius' house where he later confesses, "Truly I perceive that God shows no partiality, but in every nation anyone who fears him and does what is right is acceptable to him."[10]

In one fell swoop, the Spirit and the Word of the Lord abolish the Levitical purity laws inhibiting the full fellowship of Jews and Gentiles in the church.

Coffin was claiming that the church's traditional condemnation of homosexuality is analogous to, if not an instance of, the Levitical condemnations rendered anachronistic for the church by Peter's vision. Here he fastened on the term "abomination" ($tô\,\hat{e}b\hat{a}$), which Leviticus uses to characterize not only human eating of certain animals (11:41) but also male homosexual relations (18:22). In a brief teaching moment, Coffin noted that "abomination" generally "does not signify something intrinsically evil (like rape or theft, which are also dealt with in the Levitical code), but something that is ritually unclean." Recovering this distinction on the basis of Acts 10, Coffin was able to renounce the Levitical proscriptions of homosexuality that were preventing fellowship between straights and gays in the church; at the same time, it enabled him to thunder against promiscuity as "cruel and degrading in any sexual orientation."[11]

Four years later, on May 5, 1985, Channing E. Phillips, a former official in the Carter Administration and then Minister of Planning and Coordination at the Riverside Church, preached "On Human Sexuality." Delivered in the context of a celebration of the Lord's Supper, his sermon was occasioned by the "Statement of Openness, Inclusion, and Affirmation of

Gay/Lesbian Persons" drafted for congregational consideration by the Adult Education Committee. The statement called for the church to "recognize and embrace" lesbian/gay relationships and further declared that "Lesbian/Gay people are expected and encouraged to share in the liturgy, general life, employment and leadership of the congregation." Taking aim at this statement, Phillips reaffirmed the traditional Christian teaching that homosexuality is a deviation from the divinely intended heterosexual model and that homosexual acts are sin. Given that many of those worshiping at the Riverside Church were sympathetic to the cause of gay and lesbian liberation, it is not entirely surprising that his sermon provoked a protest demonstration even before a benediction could be pronounced.[12]

Phillips, like Coffin, arrived at his conclusions on scriptural grounds. Holding that the Bible is both "a resource on human sexuality" and "in some unique sense, the Word of God," Phillips expounded on Gen. 1:27 ("male and female he created them") and Gen. 2:24 ("Therefore, a man leaves his father and his mother and cleaves to his wife, and they become one flesh.") According to Phillips, "heterosexuality is being lifted up as the model of human sexuality," or, in the words he quoted from an unnamed theologian, "[t]he heterosexual relationship, ordained by marriage, is the *parable* of human sexuality."[13]

Furthermore, this heterosexual model derived from Genesis is not abrogated, but confirmed, by the gospel. Jesus himself employed this model as a norm when condemning all divorce as adultery in Mark 10. His "hard words" here, which are "consistent with his unrelenting demand for obedience to the will of God" as typified in the Sermon on the Mount, "imply that deviation from the parable of the heterosexual relationship ordained by marriage is contrary to God's will—is sin." Although Jesus had nothing explicit to say about homosexuality, his invoking of the normative heterosexual "model" in teaching the indissolubility of marriage implied for Phillips a negative judgment on homosexual acts. Thus, the only remedy for both homosexuals and heterosexuals engaging in sexual relations outside of heterosexual marriage is to receive forgiveness from Jesus Christ and to obey his command to "go, and sin no more" (John 8:11, KJV).[14]

The following Sunday, Mother's Day, Coffin returned both to the pulpit and to the topic of homosexuality: "I want to say a few words about my beloved colleague's sermon of last Sunday and the subsequent intervention in the service that the sermon prompted." Coffin frankly acknowledged a church divided. "What are we going to do?" he asked. "We are going to behave as those who believe in the Lord Jesus Christ." Confronting the crisis, Coffin urged his congregation to "obey the simplest, most fundamental, and difficult injunction of Scripture, we will love one another, gay and straight." The same "law of love" he had earlier seen as abrogating Levitical taboos, he now invoked as a guide for Christians embroiled in controversy.[15]

Turning to his subject, Coffin did not respond directly to Phillips's interpretation of the Genesis creation accounts. Instead, he picked a fight with the apostle Paul. He called into question Paul's branding of homosexual acts as unnatural (Rom. 1:26–27). Coffin apparently regarded Phillips's espousal of an exclusive, divinely ordained "heterosexual model" as consistent with, or equivalent to, Paul's views in Romans. By challenging Paul, Coffin could chip away at the argument of his ministerial colleague.

Coffin was aware that we use the terms "natural" and "unnatural" in a variety of ways. If we use them as they are employed, for example, by the biological or psychological sciences for speaking of the way things are empirically, then Paul by our lights was unaware of homosexual orientation. His "science" assumes everyone is "naturally" straight, so that to act otherwise is "unnatural." Then again, we may also think of "natural" or "unnatural" as cultural preferences. It is natural for Spaniards and unnatural for Norwegians to take siestas. When Paul says homosexuality is unnatural, he may mean it's something only Gentiles do. After all, Paul also thinks it unnatural for men to wear their hair long (1 Cor. 11:14). Paul is certainly entitled to his historically contingent views, but he's wrong if he's claiming that short haircuts for men, and by extension, straight sex, reflect an immutable norm.

But could the church understand what is natural in any other sense? Yes, said Coffin, "The law of love," an obvious reference to the Great Commandment, takes precedence in the church over "the laws of biology." In other words, whatever the genetic or chemical basis for homosexuality, and we might add, however negative its cultural standing, the gospel of Jesus Christ calls all persons of both sexual orientations to lives of love. The "law of love" can only regard convenantal same-sex couplings as natural. To regard them otherwise is sheer homophobia.[16]

Assessment

Having uncovered the argumentation of Channing E. Phillips and William Sloane Coffin, Jr., on homosexuality, I now assess what they have said (or left unsaid) by applying criteria typically used by theologians as tests for doctrinal faithfulness.[17] Of a number that could be employed, I have chosen three because of their special prominence in and for the practice of preaching. They are congruence with scripture, consequence, and consistency with worship.

Congruence with Scripture

Both Coffin and Phillips took care to show their positions as congruent with those of scripture. No doubt, the task of proclaiming the gospel in relation to, and on the basis of, scripture predisposes pulpit discourse to emphasize this criterion as foremost in establishing Christian teaching.

In each case, the congruence of what was preached with what scripture is saying about homosexuality was achieved indirectly by employing analogies and inferences. For example, Phillips, the traditionalist in this debate, studiously refrained from invoking or even citing the biblical prohibitions of homosexual acts in a proof-texting or biblicist fashion.[18] Likewise, Coffin, who took the reformist side, did not simply examine and then dismiss difficult texts, but he sought to interpret them by setting them into relation with other texts.[19] Thus, Phillips cannot be written off as a "fundamentalist," and Coffin cannot be dismissed as a "typical liberal." Both took seriously the overall force of the canonical context in which particular scriptural voices are situated. The texts chosen by Phillips from Genesis and Mark and Coffin's invocation of "the law of love," presumably a reference to the Great Commandment, all point to covenant fidelity as the calling of the Christian. Coffin noted the demanding character of this covenantal love by uttering a strong pulpit no to promiscuity and a strong pulpit yes to homosexuals hitherto regarded as "unclean." Phillips stressed the demanding character of this covenantal love in its exclusion of divorce, promiscuity, and homosexual acts, but he also pointed to the divine yes of God's forgiveness of all such infidelities in Jesus Christ.

What then finally divides these two positions, each seemingly congruent with scripture? By means of Acts 10, Coffin understood the "law of love" as welcoming the mutual sexual expression of covenant fidelity between persons of the same sex. Phillips, by contrast, saw the creation stories of Genesis 1 and 2, taken with Mark 10, as restricting the mutual sexual expression of covenant fidelity to married persons of the opposite sex. Despite their converging commitment to the centrality of covenant fidelity, Phillips and Coffin diverged in their conclusions as to the patterns such fidelity can take. Thus, they came to an impasse at the level of scriptural interpretation.

Consequence

If congruence with scripture as a criterion of doctrinal faithfulness is central in much Protestant theology, that of consequence is often more prominent in the newer theologies of liberation. What are the consequences of Christian teaching, especially upon the least and the last? Yet even the Second Helvetic Confession, by endorsing Augustine's "rule of faith and love," also points to the criterion of consequence.[20] Any church teaching that has the net effect of turning Christians against the apostolic gospel of love of God and neighbor is unscriptural—even if, following the devil's example in tempting our Lord, such teaching quotes the Bible chapter and verse.

Coffin employed the criterion this way:

> If what we think is right and wrong divides still further the human family, there must be something wrong with what we think is right.

Enough of this cruelty and hatred, this punitive legislation toward gay people. Peter widened his horizons; let's not narrow ours.[21]

Mel White, a former ghost writer for Pat Robertson, Jerry Falwell, and Oliver North, and now dean of the Cathedral of Hope (Metropolitan Community Church) in Dallas, built an entire sermon around the criterion of consequence. The sermon decried the traditional Christian position on homosexuality by narrating a series of tragic stories such as the following:

> Recently a senior in a southern California high school hanged himself. He was a sensitive, gifted, talented boy who wanted to be a Nazarene pastor. Then, suddenly, in the middle of the night, alone, he wrapped a sheet around his neck and died.
>
> Rumors surfaced later that the 16-year-old had been struggling with his sexuality. You and I know what that boy went through. Wanting to serve Christ but terrified of the lies of the religious right that had trickled down to his parents, his pastor, and his friends, he gave into despair and to injustice.[22]

Even those of us put off by White's fervor are compelled to consider, if we haven't already, the consequence of our teaching. Human lives are at stake, and at risk, in what we say.

In fairness to the traditionalist preachers, they too are concerned with consequences. Guy E. Wampler, who is pastorally sensitive to gays and lesbians, points to the criterion of consequence in relation to Romans 1:

> I understand what Paul writes in his letter to the Christians in Rome. I know what happens when faith breaks down: life becomes cheap; control goes haywire. It happens in some of our cities, too. I know the law, and with Paul I want order![23]

Similarly, Phillips began his Riverside sermon with a litany of sexual excesses typified by the antics of Roxanne Pulitzer and Rita Jenrette, as aired on the television talk show "Donahue." In so doing, Phillips implied that sexual permissiveness is a cultural consequence of the church's failure to uphold and to proclaim the moral law commanded by Christ.[24]

The difficulty with the criterion of consequence is that it easily turns into a blame game. What is cause and what is consequence? Are consequences amassed by anecdotal evidence, or are they evident in statistical summaries? How does one determine that church teaching is the chief culprit in causing an anti-Christian result when so many other factors are at work in human conduct and misconduct? In my judgment, no preacher can ignore the criterion of consequence, but it is not decisive for the question of what the church should proclaim regarding homosexuality.

Consistency with Worship

This criterion for doctrinal faithfulness states that the rule of prayer is a norm for belief (*lex orandi, lex credendi*). The liturgical and sacramental life of the church is seen as preceding, grounding, and contextualizing its official teaching. This criterion is often identified with the catholic "liturgical" churches, whether Eastern, Roman, or Anglican. Not surprisingly, therefore, Bishop John S. Spong appeals directly to the Episcopal baptism and confirmation rite as sanctioning the full inclusion of gays and lesbians in the membership and holy orders of the church.[25]

By contrast, the free-church liturgical heritage of Riverside, a congregation of the American Baptist Convention and the United Church of Christ (UCC), is evident in that Phillips, a UCC minister, never mentioned in his sermon that its scriptural texts were prominent in the then-current UCC marriage rite. Phillips did conclude his sermon in Reformed fashion by saying, "We are moving to the Lord's Table, where, as we renew our covenant with God and each other, we are invited 'to examine' ourselves."[26]

While Coffin made no explicit reference in his sermons to the rites of the church, a closer examination indicates that his reformist position on homosexuality was heavily indebted, perhaps more than he realized, to the rule of prayer. In his 1981 sermon, Coffin noted "the loving, lasting relations that patently exist today between so many gay people in this country, this city, *and this church.*"[27] Four years later, he spoke of how his mind was changed on homosexuality by the witness to the gospel "borne by gay and lesbian friends, whose same-sex relationships were clearly vehicles of God's humanizing intentions."[28]

As Coffin looked out from the pulpit on his gathered congregation, what he recognized, and what was new in the church as a worshiping community, was the presence and participation of lesbians and gays who were giving thanks and praise to God for their same-sex covenant partners. This is what Phillips did not discern. Phillips's preaching took no account of the prayers of the faithful, prayers whose content set aside his traditionalist condemnation. By contrast, Coffin's preaching was consistent with Christian worship. By recognizing that gays and lesbians already belong to the people of God at prayer, Coffin's sermons on the issue of homosexuality proved more faithful to the gospel—and so will ours.

Postscript

On June 2, 1985, the congregation of the Riverside Church overwhelmingly adopted the controversial reformist statement on homosexuality that had occasioned the remarkable pulpit exchanges between Phillips and Coffin. Without seeking to minimize the role of parish politics and pulpit personalities in Riverside's decision, it is instructive to note that the congregation's official action followed, rather than preceded, the preaching of the gospel. By contrast, many mainline denominations, including the Presbyterian Church (U.S.A.), are addressing the issue of homosexuality primarily in legislative and judicial contexts. This tends to overemphasize the church as a juridical institution, missing the point of the Reformation that the church is first of all that community of prayer and praise created by the preaching of the gospel. Thus, it is both salutary for the church and urgent for the resolution of the homosexuality issue that this question be resituated within the preaching and the prayers of worshiping congregations.

We may agree or disagree with the legislative action finally taken at Riverside. But we who are heirs of the Reformation cannot disagree with a process of doctrinal adjudication that emerges from the church as an evangelical event, as the liturgical assembly where the gospel, attested by scripture, is preached, heard, and enacted. For this reason, Patrick Henry's plea on the topic of homosexuality, "What we need is to hear more from the pulpit about it," remains timely. As our case study shows, such preaching, sooner or later, one way or another, does matter.

NOTES

1. Patrick Henry, "Homosexuals: Identity and Dignity," *Theology Today* 33 (1976): 33.
2. Jon M. Walton, "In Search of Sexual Ethics for the Single Life," *Pulpit Digest* 70 (1990): 46.
3. For examples, see Carl F. H. Henry, "The Fight of the Day," in *Best Sermons* vol. 1, ed. James W. Cox and Kenneth M. Cox (San Francisco: Harper & Row, 1988), 204–10; Ray C. Steadman, *From Guilt to Glory I: Hope for the Helpless* (Portland, Ore.: Multnomah, 1978).
4. For examples, see Lisa Bove, "Rejoice and Proclaim," and Daniel E. Smith, "Gay Angels?," in *Called Out: The Voices and Gifts of Lesbian, Gay, Bisexual, and Transgendered Presbyterians*, Jane A. Spahr et al., eds. (Gaithersburg, Md.: Chi Rho, 1995), 28–32, 46–49; Carter Heyward, *Our Passion for Justice: Images of Power, Sexuality, and Liberation* (New York: Pilgrim Press, 1984), 179–83, 200–210.
5. For two sermons that give eloquent first-person testimony to the power of the gospel amid ecclesiastical persecution, see Sarah Balmer, "I Came as a Person, I Left as an Issue," *More Light Update* 9, no. 3 (1988): 1–5; Scott D. Anderson, "Out of the Closet, Out of the Ministry," in *Called Out*, 65–71. The religious press recently took note of the "coming out" sermon of the Rev. Jeanne Audrey Powers. See "Methodist Official 'Comes Out,'" *The Christian Century* 112 (1995): 703–4.
6. Jim Larson, "Welcome Home: A Coming Out Sermon," *More Light Update* 12, no. 9 (1992): 13. Mary L. Foulke, Associate Pastor of the Brick Presbyterian Church, New York City, framed the issue similarly, if less existentially, in a Gay Pride Day sermon. See "Faithfulness and the Law," *More*

Light Update 11, no. 3 (1990): 1. I have tried to steer clear of two dubious assumptions inherent in Foulke's formulation: first, that the genetically given or environmentally caused can be identified, as such, with God's good creation; second, that deviation from God's good creation occurs only in the present exercising of an autonomous human will.

7. "The Second Helvetic Confession," in *The Constitution of the Presbyterian Church (U.S.A.), Part 1: Book of Confessions* (New York/Atlanta: Office of the General Assembly, 1983), 5.013. Compare "The Westminster Confession of Faith," 6.006, 6.008, 6.010.

8. Texts typically cited in this regard include Gen. 19:1–29; Lev. 18:22; 20:13; Judg. 19; Rom. 1:18–32; 1 Cor. 6:9, 1 Tim. 1:10. On the traditionalist side, see the thorough inventory and analysis of these texts by Guy E. Wampler, Jr., "The Controversy about Homosexuality: A Sermon," *Brethren Life and Thought* 39 (1994): 102–5; on the reformist side, the most complete discussion is that of Patrick Henry, "Homosexuals," 34–36, and William Sloane Coffin, Jr., "Homosexuality," *Sermons from Riverside* (July 12, 1981): 2–4.

9. Coffin, "Homosexuality," 1. Coffin's sermon was subsequently republished as "Homosexuality Revisited: Whose Problem?" in *Christianity and Crisis* 41 (1981): 290, 300–302; then (slightly revised) as "Homosexuality" in *The Courage to Love* (San Francisco: Harper & Row, 1982), 39–47; also reprinted in *Church and Society* 73, no. 2 (1982): 14–19. Quotations in this essay are taken from the original text.

10. Coffin, "Homosexuality," 1–2, 6. For subsequent sermons that also find Acts 10 to authorize the full inclusion of homosexuals in the church, see Kennedy M. McGowan, "What God Has Called Clean," *More Light Update* 10, no. 4 (1989): 1–5; John S. Spong, "The Oldest Debate in Christian History," *More Light Update* 12, no. 4 (1991): 6–12; and Jeffrey K. Krehbiel, "The Power of Relationships," *More Light Update* 13, no. 10 (1993): 11–13. Krehbiel focuses on Acts 15:8, which presupposes Acts 10.

11. Coffin, "Homosexuality," 3, 6. To place Coffin's distinction into John Calvin's language, the biblical prohibitions of homosexual acts belong to the "ceremonial law" repealed in Christ. By contrast, the prohibitions of fornication and adultery pertain to the "moral law" confirmed by Christ in the Great Commandment (Matt. 22:37–40). See *Calvin: Institutes of the Christian Religion*, part of the Library of Christian Classics, trans. Ford Lewis Battles, ed. John T. McNeill (Philadelphia: Westminster Press, 1960), 2:1503–4 (4.20.15).

12. Channing E. Phillips, "On Human Sexuality," *Sermons from Riverside* (May 5, 1985): 1–2. For the text of the statement occasioning Phillips's sermon, see "Openness, Inclusion and Affirmation: The Riverside Church Statement," *More Light Update* 6, no. 5 (1985): 4–5. For a brief account of the controversy, see "Gays and Riverside," *The Christian Century* 102 (1985): 576–77.

13. Phillips, 2–3.

14. Ibid., 2–5. Hence, celibacy is assumed for Christians of homosexual orientation. Unlike Adam, it is good that they are alone! This conclusion, inherent in the traditionalist argument, leaves at least one of its advocates uneasy. See Wampler, 104.

15. Coffin, "The Fundamental Injunction: Love One Another," *Sermons from Riverside* (May 12, 1985): 1–2. See also Coffin, "Homosexuality," 4–5 on the "law of love."
16. Coffin, "Fundamental Injunction," 1–3; compare Coffin, "Homosexuality," 4–6.
17. See Christopher Morse, *Not Every Spirit: A Dogmatics of Christian Disbelief* (Valley Forge, Pa.: Trinity Press International, 1994), 45–70.
18. This is also true of traditionalists Guy E. Wampler and Earle W. Fike, Jr. See the latter's, "Together without Conformity: A Sermon," *Brethren Life and Thought* 39, no. 2 (1994): 110–11.
19. For a sermon that virtually abandons scripture on behalf of a more accepting stance by the church, see Richard E. Hamilton, "Difficult Choices: The Christian and the Homosexual," in *Preaching the Topical Sermon*, ed. Ronald J. Allen (Louisville, Ky.: Westminster John Knox Press, 1992), 128–37.
20. See "The Second Helvetic Confession," 5.010. See also Saint Augustine, *On Christian Doctrine*, trans. D. W. Robertson (New York/London: Macmillan Co., 1958), 30–32.
21. Coffin, "Homosexuality," 6.
22. Mel White, "Jesus Acted Up!," *More Light Update* 14, no. 8 (1994): 15. See also 12–13.
23. Wampler, 104. Nevertheless, Wampler readily concedes the tragic historical consequences of certain scripture passages.
24. Phillips, 1–2. Fike also fears the homosexual controversy will have the consequence of a "covenant-shattering confrontation" for the Church of the Brethren. He therefore subordinates the resolution of the homosexuality issue to that of church unity. Spong takes exactly the opposite view. Compare Fike, 111–12, and Spong, 8, 11–12.
25. Spong, 7, 11–12. For a recent Protestant discussion that insightfully relates the "rule of prayer" (*lex orandi*) to the issue of homosexuality, see Morse, 54, 281–82.
26. Phillips, 5.
27. Coffin, "Homosexuality," 3–4 (emphasis added).
28. Coffin, "Fundamental Injunction," 3.

Part 3

How Do We Live Faithfully?

10
The Pastoral Dilemma

Thomas W. Gillespie

The story is told of a senator who was running for reelection. On the stump in his home state, he was asked about his position on a particularly controversial bill then pending before the Congress. "Some of my friends are for it, and some of my friends are against it," he responded, "but I want you to know that I am for my friends." He won the election in a landslide.

The humor of this fictional anecdote is predicated on the cynical assumption that elected public officials are more interested in winning votes than they are in deciding difficult issues. A more charitable reading, however, might allow for the inference that the senator was more concerned about people than principles, about relationships than arguments. In the ethos of contemporary American society, the latter interpretation is not only possible but increasingly probable.

Thus, when unavoidable controversial issues affect people we know and care about, as is the case in the current public and ecclesial debate on homosexuality, the human factor is crucial in the disputation. Those who seek love in same-sex relationships are people—sometimes family or colleagues, or as with pastors, members of our congregation. Thomas E. Schmidt reminds us of the importance of the personal dimension of the issue in his recent book *Straight & Narrow? Compassion and Clarity in the Homosexuality Debate:*

> These are people with faces, people with names, often Christian people, and whatever we conclude about the larger issues their stories represent, we must never lose sight of their individual struggles, their individual pain, their faces. If we neglect faces, we neglect the gospel.[1]

In that concluding sentence, Professor Schmidt articulates the pastoral dilemma. How shall I deal with this issue in such a way that I neglect neither the faces of the homosexual people I know and care about nor the gospel of Jesus Christ? Put positively, how shall I, as a minister of the gospel, serve the homosexual people I know (and don't know) in my congregation?

Paul and the Saving Power of the Gospel

My understanding of the gospel, as well as that of the Reformed theological tradition in which I stand, has been shaped in no small measure by the canonical letters of the apostle Paul. In Rom. 1:16, he declares programmatically that the gospel is "the power of God unto salvation for everyone who has faith, to the Jew first and also to the Greek." The gospel is power, God's power, God's saving power. From what then does the gospel save us? Paul argues in Romans that the gospel delivers us from: (1) the power of sin to oppress us (Romans 6); (2) the power of the Law to condemn us (Romans 7); and (3) the power of death to hold us (Romans 8). Those thus liberated are declared *just* before God, and in their liberation God demonstrates his own *justice.* "For in [the gospel] the justice of God is revealed" (Rom. 1:17).

With regard to the oppression of sin, Paul gives examples elsewhere of the gospel's liberating power. Of special interest is a text that relates the power of the gospel explicitly to the issue of homosexuality, 1 Cor. 6:9–11. The literary location of this brief passage is a section of 1 Corinthians (5:1–6:20) in which the apostle is addressing two instances of behavior in the Corinthian congregation that do not honor the gospel, one a matter of incest (5:1–13) and the other a case of fraud (6:1–11). In speaking to these matters, Paul introduces a series of "vice catalogues" (as they are called in New Testament scholarship) that give specificity to the ways in which sin evidences itself as an oppressive force in human life (5:10, 11, and 6:9–10).[2] In the first (5:10) he lists the sexually immoral, the greedy, robbers, and idolators. In the second (5:11) he repeats this list and adds to it revilers and drunkards. In the third (6:9–10) he warns that "wrongdoers will not inherit the kingdom of God" and identifies the endangered as all those previously mentioned, plus thieves. Further, the sexually immoral are now specified as fornicators, adulterers, male prostitutes, and sodomites.[3]

Before stating the point that I wish to make from this third vice catalogue, however, it is imperative that we notice two important features of these three lists. The first is that sexual sins are not singled out for exclusive attention, but are conjoined with sins of economic injustice (perpetrated in a variety of ways by the greedy, robbers, and thieves) and the sin of religious idolatry. The second notable feature of these lists is that sexual immorality is specified first as heterosexual fornication and adultery, and only then is it further identified as homosexual behavior; which is to say that the latter is no lesser or greater an instance of sin than the former.

Unfortunately, in my judgment 1 Cor. 6:9–11 has been used in the debate on homosexuality primarily to establish the biblical view that same-gender sex is sinful. What is often neglected is the concluding verse, which attests to the power of the gospel to liberate people from conditions and consequences of behavior that is subject to divine indictment. The text reads:

> And this is what some of you used to be. But you were washed, you were sanctified, you were justified in the name of the Lord Jesus Christ and in the Spirit of our God.
>
> (1 Cor. 6:11)

Imagine such a congregation. Not *all*, to be sure, but *some* nonetheless were—in their pre-Christian lives—greedy, robbers and thieves. Some were drunkards and revilers. And, yes, some were fornicators, adulterers, male prostitutes, and sodomites. That was then, however. The *past tense of the verb* is crucial to our understanding of what the apostle is saying: "And this is what some of you *were*." Now the situation is different. These very people were *washed, sanctified,* and *justified* in the name of the Lord Jesus Christ and in the Spirit of God.

Gordon D. Fee calls this text "one of the more important theological statements in the epistle."[4] He explains:

> As in 1:30, the three verbs are primarily metaphors of salvation, each expressing a special facet of their conversion in light of the preceding sentences: they had been "washed" from the filth of their former life-styles expressed in the preceding list; they had been "sanctified," set apart by God for holy, godly living that stands in stark contrast to their former wickedness; though formerly "unjust," they had been justified, so that now right with God they may inherit the kingdom that before they could not. . . . Finally, since the three verbs refer to the same reality, and since each of them has "God" as the implied subject, the two prepositional phrases are to be understood as modifying all three verbs. The latent Trinitarianism of the sentence, therefore, is difficult to escape. God has effected salvation "in the name of the Lord Jesus Christ and by the Spirit."[5]

The significance of this exegetical commentary on 1 Cor. 6:11 is its assurance that here we are not skating near the blue ice of the canon where its central witness to the gospel is thin. Rather, that witness is firmly attested in terms of the gospel's cleansing, sanctifying, and justifying power to effect transformation of human life, including, and in particular, its moral character. Idolatry, greed and thievery, fornication and adultery may be deeply ingrained patterns of human conduct, but they are not *necessary* patterns because of the gospel. The same is true, Paul attests, of those given to same-gender sex. Evidently, there were faces in the Corinthian church whose experience of the gospel confirmed the apostle's assertion.

Undergirding and informing this apostolic statement of the need for and the possibility of homosexual transformation is the biblical understanding of creation. What qualifies homosexual liaisons for inclusion on Paul's vice list is stipulated in his discussion of this topic in Rom. 1:26–27. Put simply, they are "against nature" (Greek *para physin*, v. 26). The apostle is speaking here, of course, in the idiom of the Stoics. But the term *nature*, as used here, is if not *baptized* by Paul the Christian, then at least *circumcised* by Paul, the Hellenistic Jew. For the Hellenistic Jew characteristically filtered Stoic terms through the medium of Jewish monotheism and thus identified *nature* with God's Law and creative intention.[6]

Two comments by German New Testament ethicist Wolfgang Schrage are pertinent here. The first is that in Rom. 1:26 "*physis* designates what is consonant with the order of creation." The second is that for Paul, "marriage is consonant with the created order."[7] The divine intention for human sexual relations, as attested in the Genesis accounts of creation and affirmed by Jesus, is the union of male and female in marriage (Gen. 2:24; see also Matt. 19:1–6).[8] It is this norm that makes homosexual behavior (as well as fornication and adultery) for Paul "a tragic distortion of the created order."[9] It is this distortion (among others) that God transforms by the power of the gospel to cleanse, sanctify and justify (1 Cor. 6:11). Such, in brief, is the pastoral response of the apostle Paul to the faces of those he knew and cared about who engaged in homosexual practice.

An Alternate View

Others today view homosexuality and its practice quite differently, however. They, too, look at the faces of homosexual people and speak to them of God's liberation from oppression. The difference is that here liberation is understood in terms of freedom not from homosexual behavior but from the stigma imposed upon such acts by a 4000-year-old Judeo-Christian moral tradition that is no longer tenable, as well as from the political, social, and ecclesial oppression of homosexual people, which that tradition has imposed and reinforced. Thus, the authentic pastoral response is to revise the public perception of homosexuality as immoral practice.

Such a revision is warranted, it is argued, by a proper reading of scripture and modern scientific knowledge about homosexuality. Because it is the scientific data that occasion the need to reinterpret scripture, I will review briefly the state of this discussion before addressing the biblical arguments.

What do we know about homosexuality today that Paul did not know, making his view of the phenomenon hopelessly naive? Specifically, what do we know scientifically about the etiology of homosexuality that renders the biblical view itself obsolete? The answer is that there is much learned speculation, an abundance of theory, and no assured knowledge.

Consider as an example the state of research into the possible biological basis of homosexuality. Published studies have focused upon structures of the brain, hormones, and genes, showing results that are, respectively, mixed, negative, and inconclusive.[10] The current state of the research, according to Columbia University psychiatrists William Byne and Bruce Parsons, is as follows:

> There is no evidence at present to substantiate a biologic theory, just as there is no compelling evidence to support any singular psychosocial explanation. While all behavior must have an ultimate biologic substrate, the appeal of current biologic explanations may derive more from dissatisfaction with the present status of psychosocial explanations than from a substantiating body of experimental data. Critical review shows the evidence favoring a biologic theory to be lacking.[11]

This professional assessment will astonish those who are under the impression given by the media that the genetic origin of homosexuality is an assured result of scientific research.

Readers may be equally surprised by the reference here to possible "psychosocial" explanations of homosexuality. For it is well known that the American Psychiatric Association (APA) removed homosexuality from its list of psychopathological disorders in 1973. What is not so well known, however, is that the action was occasioned not by a change of scientific understanding of homosexuality, but by the internal and external political pressures exerted upon the APA.[12] A subsequent survey (1977) found that 69 percent of the psychiatrists polled held that homosexuality "usually represents a pathological adaptation" in human development.[13]

What the biological and psychological explanations of the cause of homosexuality have in common is the conviction that the homosexual person has *no choice* in regard to the gender of his or her erotic attraction. That was decided at conception (the genetic theory) or in infancy (the psychological theory). Thus, the nuclear core of homosexuality is never an act of will, never a conscious choice. It is this deterministic view that informs the concept of sexual identity or *orientation*.

Yet biological and psychological theories are not alone on the table of proposals regarding the cause of homosexuality. Social constructionist theory, for example, summarily dismisses the concept of a *given* orientation in favor of the explanation that sexual identity and behavior are learned. In a review of David Greenberg's massive study, *The Construction of Homosexuality*,[14] Don Browning underscores the radical character of the author's social constructionist thesis "that homosexuality is not a static condition; it is not like being black or white or left-handed." The popular notion that homosexual behavior is a manifestation of some inner essence, biologically or psychologically determined, is "anachronistic" according to Greenberg. Rather, homosexuality is learned behavior, produced and interpreted in different ways by different societies at different times.

Browning also notes that "Greenberg's work challenges the presuppositions of nearly all recent discussions of homosexuality in both Protestant and Catholic churches" because "these churches in recent years have adopted some version of the *essentialist* view of homosexuality" in their official statements.[15] The point is worthy of emphasis because it is precisely this essentialist assumption that determines the view of those in the current ecclesial debate who seek the liberation of homosexual people from moral stigma and its resultant oppression rather than from immoral behavior. They accept as fact the assumption that homosexuality is something people *are* before it is something they *do*. Because sexual orientation does not entail choice, it is amoral by definition. Morality becomes an issue only in the way a given sexual orientation is exercised. Thus, a great deal, if not literally everything, depends upon the essentialist assumption. My point here is that it remains only an assumption. The question of the etiology of homosexuality is far from settled.

Revisionist Strategies

Christians whose views on homosexuality are predicated upon the essentialist assumption are aware that the testimony of the Bible on this subject is limited but consistent. Wherever homosexual acts are mentioned in scripture, they are indicated. This problem has been addressed in three ways: (1) revise the sense of the texts; (2) discount the significance of the texts; and (3) critique the validity of the texts in the light of more central biblical themes.

The first strategy seeks to revise the sense of biblical statements about homosexuality in a manner that limits their meaning to acts that do not include certain kinds of homosexual relations as we know them today. Thus 1 Cor. 6:9–10 is read as a vice list that includes child prostitutes and adult pedophiles rather than male prostitutes and sodomites. What is indicated is thus pederasty and prostitution, not homosexual relations per se.[16] Similarly, Rom. 1:26–27 is interpreted as a condemnation of homosexual liaisons between heterosexual women and men who, respectively, "exchanged" and "gave up" intercourse "natural" to their sexual identity, not between people of homosexual orientation, thus leaving open the question of authentic same-sex love.[17] Since others have responded critically to the revisionist readings of these two texts,[18] I will note only that the imposition of the concept of sexual orientation on Paul is anachronistic, and the arguments fail that Paul, in either text, objects to anything other than same-sex coitus itself.

The second strategy qualifies the significance of texts in such a manner that their applicability to the Christian life is eliminated. Lev. 18:22 and 20:13 are located (properly) in the so-called Holiness Code of Israel (Leviticus 17—26) and thereby dismissed (improperly) as moral guidance on the grounds that (1) the Code is concerned about ritual purity rather than morality, and (2) Christians have been released from purity regulations by Jesus (Mark 7:1–8), as well as Paul (Romans 14).[19]

The issue is not whether the Holiness Code is concerned with ritual purity, however; it is whether the concept of purity is informed by substantive moral considerations that carry over into the New Testament. It should be noted that Leviticus 18 and 20 alone afford parallel prohibitions of such moral actions as incest (18:6–18; 20:11–12, 7, 19–21), adultery (18:20; 20:10), child sacrifice (18:21; 20:2–5), and bestiality (18:23; 20:15–16). The bridge chapter (Leviticus 19) prohibits theft and false dealing (v. 11), oppression of neighbors and robbery (v. 13), injustice (v. 15), and commands provision for the poor (v. 9), concern for the deaf and the blind (v. 14), justice in the market place (vv. 35–36), and the love of neighbor as self (v. 18)—the law designated by Jesus as second only to the commandment to love God (Matt. 22:36–40).

If the concern of the Levitical Holiness Code is ritual purity, which it is, then such purity is morally informed and qualified in large measure. Paul certainly assumes this in 1 Cor. 6:11 where he declares that the gospel effects a sanctity or holiness in believers that is characterized by its freedom from the moral vices listed in v. 9 and 10. Further, 1 Cor. 6:9–11 illustrates how the moral concerns of the law continued to inform the apostle's ethical sensitivities long after he had denied the law a salvific function. The vices listed in v. 9 and 10 have their precedent in the Holiness Code itself.[20] Thus, the relation between purity and morality in the scriptures is not as neat and tidy as the revisionists suggest.

In the final analysis, however, the results of these efforts are rendered moot by the third strategy, which is informed more by hermeneutical than by exegetical considerations. What this entails may be illustrated by two examples.

One is the so-called Acts 10 argument.[21] An analogy is claimed here between the status of Gentiles in the first-century church and the ecclesial status of homosexual people today. The story line in Acts 10 runs like this: Peter is told in a trance dream that Gentiles are no longer to be considered "unclean," and thus they are eligible to hear the gospel. This is then confirmed by the conversion of Cornelius and his household, accompanied by their receiving the Holy Spirit. From this, the inference is drawn that because homosexual Christians have received the Spirit, God is now telling us that they, too, should no longer be considered "unclean" and thus worthy of full inclusion in the church and its ordained offices. Clearly, homosexual Christians have received the Holy Spirit and are included in the church. But the issue regarding ordination is not purity (confirmed by the Spirit); it is morality (conformed to the Spirit). The Spirit can be both "quenched" (1 Thess. 5:19) and "grieved" (Eph. 4:30).[22]

A second example is provided by George Edwards in his *Gay/Lesbian Liberation: A Biblical Perspective*, which explicitly adopts a hermeneutic informed by "perspectives from gay/lesbian liberation theology."[23] What this means and how it works is illustrated by his discussion of the confrontation between Paul and Peter at Antioch over table fellowship between Jewish and Gentile Christians in a mixed church (Gal. 2:11–21). Edwards makes two moves here that typify the liberationist hermeneutic. First, he identifies the controlling *center* of Paul's theology as "justification by faith," a divine action in Jesus Christ that liberates believers from the requirements of "legal rectitude" and yet obligates them to "act out basic cultural implications of the liberationist mandate of the gospel." His second move is to assert that the issue of table fellowship at Antioch is analogous to the issue of homosexuality in the church today. It is Paul's position that "Peter's cultural captivity to ethnic chauvinism must be overcome"; even so, "the liberationist solution to the issue of homosexual exclusion is a necessary corollary of this same premise."[24]

The establishment of the center of Paul's theology is standard hermeneutical practice in the Reformed tradition, which has long honored the concept of the *scopus* of scripture and has identified it with Jesus Christ.[25] It is the second move made by Edwards that is problematic. The analogy Edwards sees between the issues of table fellowship and homosexuality is predicated upon the assumption that both are matters of cultural prejudice. This assumption is crucial to the case Edwards makes for their analogous resolution. Cultural matters are relative and thus changeable. Since Paul's views on homosexuality are cultural rather than theological, they are subject to correction by the gospel itself. Thus, Rom. 1:26–27 is dismissed as a cultural artifact that typifies the views of Hellenistic Judaism[26]—views that are no longer tenable, given what is known today about homosexuality.

One of the virtues of liberation theology, according to Edwards, is that it "sustains serious connection with the biblical roots of both Judaism and Christianity" while providing "intelligent correlation of cognitive and sociological categories of human existence."[27] The virtue can become a vice, however, if theology develops what Paul Sigmund calls "an undue dependence" upon social science theory, as liberation theology is prone to do.[28] This is clearly the case with Edwards, who accepts uncritically the essentialist assumption and allows it to dominate the discussion.[29] As Edwards concedes in a concluding prediction, the liberation of homosexual people that he envisions "will take place only when the historic biblical prohibitions that we have discussed are brought into *responsible relationship with contemporary sexology.*"[30] In this context, responsible means subservient. But why biblical interpretation should yield to unproven scientific theory, such as the essentialist view of homosexuality, is the unanswered question.

Conclusion

How then should the pastoral dilemma be resolved? Given my assessment of the issues entailed in the debate over homosexuality, I am compelled to draw two conclusions. First, because the gospel is "the power of God unto salvation" (Rom. 1:16), I am faithful to the faces of the people I know and care about when I tell them the gospel truth: that the power of the triune God is at work in and through the good news of Jesus Christ to liberate all from the oppression of sin, whether their particular vices are sexual or nonsexual, and, if the former, whether they are heterosexual or homosexual in kind. Second, because "the justice of God is revealed" in the gospel (Rom. 1:17), I am faithful to those same faces when I seek to overcome every form of systemic injustice that oppresses human life.

NOTES

1. Thomas E. Schmidt, *Straight & Narrow? Compassion & Clarity in the Homosexuality Debate* (Downers Grove, Ill.: InterVarsity, 1995), 11.
2. Wolfgang Schrage, "Vices are not petty offenses but signs of human sinfulness . . . " *The Ethics of the New Testament* (Philadelphia: Fortress Press, 1988), 129. For other examples of such lists in the Pauline corpus, see 2 Cor. 12:20–21; Gal. 5:19–21; Rom. 1:29–31; Col. 3:5, 8; Eph. 5:3–5; 1 Tim. 1:9–11; 2 Tim. 3:2–5; Tit. 3:3; see also Mark 7:21–22; 1 Peter 2:1; 4:3; Rev. 21:8; 22:15.
3. The terminology here is from the New Revised Standard Version, as are all citations from the biblical text.
4. Gordon D. Fee, *The First Epistle to the Corinthians* (Grand Rapids: Wm. B. Eerdmans Publishing Co., 1987), 245.
5. Ibid., 246.
6. Richard B. Hays, "Relations Natural and Unnatural: A Response to John Boswell's Exegesis of Romans 1," *The Journal of Religious Ethics* 14 (1986): 196.
7. Schrage, 204–5.
8. For an insightful discussion of marriage as "a natural institution of which the New Testament has a good deal to say," see Oliver O'Donovan, *Resurrection and Moral Order: An Outline for Evangelical Ethics* (Grand Rapids: Wm. B. Eerdmans Publishing Co., 1986), 69–71.
9. Hays, 207.
10. See the comprehensive survey of the scientific literature on this subject in Schmidt, 137–42 (see the extensive bibliography, 231–36).
11. William Byne and Bruce Parsons, "Human Sexual Orientation: The Biologic Theories Reappraised," *Archives of General Psychiatry* 50 (1993): 228 (cited by Schmidt, 140).
12. The process that led to this decision in December of 1973 is documented by Charles W. Socarides, "Sexual Politics and Scientific Logic: The Issue of Homosexuality," *The Journal of Psychohistory* 10 (1992): 307–29; see also Stanton L. Jones and Don E. Workman, "Homosexuality: The Behavioral Sciences and the Church, *Journal of Psychology and Theology* 17 (1989): 214–15.
13. Ronald Bayer, *Homosexuality and American Psychiatry: The Politics of Diagnosis* (New York: Basic Books, 1981), 167.

14. David Greenberg, *The Construction of Homosexuality* (Chicago: The University of Chicago Press, 1988), 635.
15. Ibid., 914 (emphasis added).
16. Robin Scroggs, *The New Testament and Homosexuality* (Philadelphia: Fortress Press, 1983), 62–65.
17. John Boswell, *Christianity, Social Tolerance, and Homosexuality* (New Haven: Yale University, 1980), 109–13.
18. Hays, 184–215. Also David F. Wright, "Homosexuals or Prostitutes? The Meaning of *Arsenokoitai* (1 Cor. 6:9; 1 Tim. 1:10)," *Vigilae Christianae* 38 (1984): 125–53.
19. L. William Countryman, *Dirt, Greed and Sex* (Philadelphia: Fortress Press, 1988), 98–123, uses this argument to explain the apostle's rhetorical strategy in Rom. 1:26–27, a text he reads as a reference to impurity rather than to morality.
20. Schrage, *The Ethics of the New Testament*, 206, finds in Paul "a dialectical attitude" toward the moral authority of the Old Testament—authoritative and yet appropriated critically through Christ and the law of love.
21. See Jeffrey S. Siker, "How to Decide? Homosexual Christians, the Bible, and Gentile Inclusion," *Theology Today* 51 (1994): 219–34.
22. See the response to Siker by Christopher R. Seitz, "Human Sexuality: Viewed from the Bible's Understanding of the Human Condition," *Theology Today* 52 (1995): 240 n. 3.
23. George A. Edwards, *Gay/Lesbian Liberation: A Biblical Perspective* (New York: Pilgrim Press, 1984), 70.
24. Ibid., 76.
25. The Dutch Calvinist G. C. Berkower, *Studies in Dogmatics: Holy Scripture* (Grand Rapids: Wm. B. Eerdmans Publishing Co., 1975), states "that Scripture is not composed of a number of isolated words, theses, and truths, but *a centered witness*" to Jesus Christ (178 [emphasis added]; see also 44).
26. Edwards, 72–74, 85–100.
27. Ibid., 77.
28. Paul E. Sigmund, *Liberation Theology at the Crossroads: Democracy or Revolution* (New York: Oxford University, 1990), 8.
29. Edwards, 99: "the theology of gay/lesbian liberation . . . assumes the naturalness to some people of same-sex orientation and acting . . . ."
30. Ibid., 100 (emphasis added).

11
Disciples Together, Constantly

A.K.M. Adam

Several years ago, the leadership of the Episcopal Church undertook a parish-based study of human sexuality. The House of Bishops sought guidance from all Episcopalians regarding the theological status of nonmarital sexual intimacy. When my own home parish discussed what the church should say about homosexuality and sexual activity outside marriage, participants in the discussion group frequently expressed annoyance with the entire process. "Why does God care about who I sleep with?" Some responded to their own question with the words of the old song, "Ain't nobody's business but my own," even though such a stance presumptuously banishes the God to whom (in the words of the Anglican Collect for Purity) "all hearts are open, all desires are known, and from whom no secrets are hid" from involvement in our sexual lives. Other participants flattened the complexity of theological deliberation into a bald assertion that "if the Bible says it, we have to do it."[1]

Neither party, however, exercised the gift and vocation of theological discernment to justify their arguments. They ignored the initial question ("Why does God care?") and simply claimed either that God was irrelevant to their sexual behavior or that God had established unambiguous guidelines for God's own reasons. Their impulse to ask why God cares was wiser, though, than their conclusions. Whatever we have to say about God's will for our sexual lives, we ought to be able to give some account of what God's interest might be in our intimate relationships.

One common answer draws on the Levitical rationale, "you must be holy as I [God] am holy." This has the merit of strong scriptural support, but it unfortunately defers the question more than it answers it; we are still left wondering what makes some forms of sexual behavior holy, others unholy, and what that has to do with God's own holiness. We may, as an alternative, draw on the scriptural natural-law tradition[2] to argue that only "natural" sex is theologically legitimate, although this approach entails problems of its own. Yet a third position submits that lesbian and gay Christians have a right to equal access to sacramental blessings of their relationships.

All three responses presuppose that the relevant question is, What are we to say about homosexuality and sexual activity outside marriage? Such a starting point, however, obscures the importance of understanding the ethical status of *all* intimate human relationships. My own approach seeks the basis for our sexual ethics in the character of relationships that God initiates and commends to us: Our relationships with all people should conform to God's relationship with Jesus, Israel, and the church. On this account, we are called to make our relationships with one another honest, faithful, self-giving, and constant. This proposal recognizes the theological soundness of some relationships that the churches now condemn, and puts hard questions to some relationships that the churches now bless; but it provides a scriptural basis for assessing the various dimensions of human sexuality, and offers a way forward that depends neither on a breezy acceptance of secular standards nor on the perpetuation of ecclesiastical ethical habits that could be subject to faithful reformation.

The first option, which stresses the holiness of certain specified sexual practices, has the benefit of relative clarity. It has likewise been adopted into the law codes of many civil jurisdictions. This position appeals to the injunctions against same-sex intimacy in Lev. 18:22: "You shall not lie with a male as with a woman" (see also Lev. 20:13). While there is much to be said concerning this verse, in this context its chief drawback is that it lacks a clear theological rationale. The Levitical dictum identifies itself clearly as God's will but does not amplify the character of that will apart from God's holiness. Some readers will find this an advantage inasmuch as this distinct statement of God's will may be less subject to interpretive quibbling. At the same time, however, even the compendious laws of sexual holiness fail to consider some sexual practices (same-sex intimacy among women, for one example). Moreover, the statutes of Levitical holiness also demand a panoply of dietary and social practices that contemporary Christians no longer feel obliged to honor. If, for instance, the Levitical taboo on male homosexual relations is eternally binding, there is no obvious reason that we should permit crossbreeding of animals or blending fabrics (Lev. 19:19), having tattoos (Lev. 19:28), sabbath-breaking (Lev. 19:3, 23:3), or any landholding beyond the limits of the fifty-year jubilee (except, of course, in walled cities; Leviticus 25). The Holiness Code makes no distinction between jubilary economics and normative heterosexuality: both are equally manifestations of God's holiness. The strength of the holiness law should be its absoluteness, but it appears that holiness is still not a sufficient ethical criterion for outlawing homosexual intimacy. Those who would appeal to the law to prohibit homosexual intimacy need supplemental legislation to cover certain sexual acts and, likewise, need a theoretical justification for adopting some absolutes from the Holiness Code while utterly disregarding others.

The second option, the tradition that draws its warrants from what we might call "natural law," entails its own complications. Does "natural" refer to a scientifically definable principle, or to God's intention for creation? If the former, we must admit that nature's message on homosexual intimacy is lamentably equivocal; scientists have attained no clarity in their efforts to discern what natural sexual relations might be.[3] Partisans of every position accuse their opponents of permitting ideological considerations to taint the scientific precision of their research. If "natural" identifies "God's will for creation" in a way that may conflict with the conclusions of the empirical sciences, we need to articulate what the relation is between God's will and nature, and how we ascertain what God's will might be. In either case, a natural-law approach leaves us without a clear answer to the question of which *aspect* of our sexual behavior warrants God's commendation or condemnation.

The third approach, which treats Christian sexual ethics as a matter of human rights, has tremendous appeal in the cultural climate of liberal democracy. One can appeal to Pauline texts such as Gal. 3:28 and Col. 3:11, to the effect that distinctions such as male and female, slave and free, Jew and Gentile, and (in this case) gay and straight are irrelevant to those who have been made one in the body of Christ. This approach begs the question, however. This view of sexuality *presupposes* that homosexuality is simply given, as is biological gender or ethnic identity. But those who resist ecclesiastical accommodation to homosexual activity argue that it is a form of behavior contrary to God's will for humanity. The voices for normative heterosexuality may point out that one would not say, "in Christ there is neither perpetrator of violence nor victim, neither oppressor nor oppressed." Moreover, the entire matter of "human rights" is complicated for disciples of a Christ who renounced his privileges and came as a slave to serve humanity. Finally, however, this "ecclesiastical rights" argument—like the other perspectives we have scanned—fails to clarify what interest God has in our intimate relationships, and so it effectively leaves Christians speechless when they are called upon to give an account of the ethical judgments they make.

Why *does* God care about our relationships? First, God cares because the character of our relationships with one another is inseparable from the character of our relationship with God. This is one implication of Jesus' teaching in the gospel of Matthew. There Jesus teaches us that in showing hospitality to others, we show hospitality to him; in clothing the naked, feeding the hungry, visiting the prisoners, we do the same to Jesus (Matthew 25). We cannot be hardhearted to our neighbors and warmhearted to God; we cannot be fickle to our loved ones and faithful to God.

The intensity and intimacy of a relationship increases its importance as a barometer of our relation to God. Thus, God cares about our relationships with one another because God cares about our relationship with God.

The church has conventionally subjected extramarital relationships to ethical scrutiny while it has regarded marriage itself as a known and approved condition. I suggest, however, that we examine all relationships of human intimacy together. If we limit our deliberation about sexual behavior only to extramarital relationships, we introduce a persistent distortion into our ethical deliberation. On one hand, marital relationships can provide crucial evidence for theologically validated human intimacy; on the other hand, marriage does not guarantee that a given relationship is sound, since marriage can in some cases simply provide a façade of legitimacy for a superficial or even malignant relationship.

When we opt to make marriage—rather than nonmarital relationships—the starting point for deliberating about the ethical status of intimate relationships, we have direct testimony attributed to Jesus and Paul. The synoptic gospels (Matthew, Mark, and Luke) show Jesus addressing the topic of marriage on two occasions: the first, when he discusses divorce; the second, when he confronts the Sadducees concerning levirate marriage (the obligation of a widow's brother-in-law to beget a son for her, so that her family would have a male heir). Paul discusses marriage in a tremendous variety of contexts, from the binding force of the law to mixed marriages to apostolic privilege. One striking feature of these various discussions is that the theological weight in each case falls on marriage's character as a commitment that binds two people together for life.

Indeed, Jesus and Paul stress both the importance of and the limitations of the lifetime commitment. Those who take marriage vows are making a lifelong commitment: "They are no longer two, but one flesh. Therefore what God has joined together, let no one separate" (Matt. 19:6). Paul likewise emphasizes that marriage is indissoluble in 1 Corinthians 7 (where he repudiates divorce in vv. 10–11) and in Rom. 7:2–3. By the same token, marriage is a strictly mundane matter ("Those who belong to this age marry and are given in marriage," Luke 20:34); widows and widowers are released from their obligation to their spouses, and marital obligations are not pertinent to the eschatological (that is, ultimate) dimension of human existence ("those who are considered worthy of a place in that age and in the resurrection from the dead neither marry nor are given in marriage. Indeed they cannot die anymore, because they are like angels and are children of God, being children of the resurrection," Luke 20:35–36). Paul seems to imagine that his preference for celibacy is a sort of preparation for this nonconjugal heavenly life. In short, marriage is ordained as a terrestrial institution, binding for life upon those who undertake it, but its jurisdiction does not extend to the heavenly dimension of believers' lives.

Now, when Paul and Jesus make the point that marriage is lifelong, they do so not as a casual digression or a simple illustration. They take the institution of marriage—itself a condition commended by God in creation but blended in a peculiar amalgam with a secular institution familiar in the political life of most societies—and anchor its theological significance in the rationale of unity and constancy that they know from the book of Genesis. In the gospels and letters, the leaders of the early church thus articulate a crucial theological justification for their approach to marriage. Marriage involves the spouses in the creation of a new relational identity that is given, sustained, and sealed by God. This new relation has a variety of civic and pragmatic dimensions (defining units of population, production, and dependency, the generation and sustenance of offspring, and so on), but its principal theological dimension is constituted by lifelong fidelity: "Therefore a man leaves his father and his mother and clings to his wife, and they become one flesh. Therefore what God has joined together, let no one separate." People whom God joins in marriage cannot—on their own initiative—break the bond of marriage, any more than humans can annul God's covenant with Israel. Indeed,the marital covenant is an icon of the covenant of grace between God and humanity, as the force of marriage metaphors in scripture illustrate (Isa. 54:5; 62:1–5; Jer. 3; Ezek. 16:8; Hos. 2:19, 20; Mal. 2:11;[4] likewise, the metaphors of Christ as spouse of all believers: Matt. 9:15; 25:1–6; John 3:29; 2 Cor. 11:2; Eph. 5:25–27; Rev. 19:7; 21:2, 9.

In other words, scripture repeatedly makes the theological point that relations of utmost human intimacy ought to communicate something about God's relation to humanity. The particular point that permeates biblical uses of the analogy of marriage most completely is that God's love for God's people is manifest in a constant, undying commitment;[5] so our relationships with one another, when we avow them in a theological context, should be constant and undying. If we shortchange the powerful testimony of Jesus and Paul to the importance of constancy in our most intimate relationships, we betray an opportunity to testify by our lives to God's avowed commitment to us.

God's commitment to us is not based on gender distinction; when God espouses Israel, when Jesus is bridegroom to the church, they do not commit themselves only to people of one gender. God's call to discipleship and concomitant promise of salvation are offered to all people. Though in the past (and in some quarters, today), full participation in the body of Christ was conditional upon maleness, many churches have recognized that women also have places in ordained ministry and church leadership. So too, full participation in church life has hitherto been limited to people with (real or feigned) heterosexual inclinations, though the gifts and the calling of God do not depend on the gender of the people to whom the disciple is sexually attracted. On the contrary, God makes a vow of covenanted constancy to *all* who are willing to receive that covenant, as the biblical writers repeatedly illustrate with the metaphor of God marrying God's people. The significance of marriage as a biblical metaphor lies in the assumption that the marital relation epitomizes the quality of mutual intimacy and fidelity in human relationship. When we see married disciples of Jesus living lives of shared commitment to one another and to the gospel, we encounter one of the most vivid material illustrations of God's faithful love for us.

On this account, the central theological importance of marriage—as the church's institution for the blessing and support of human intimacy—lies in *constancy*. Only our trust in God's constancy can make possible the radical commitment that accepts Jesus' call to discipleship (calling us to give over every element of our lives in the service of our sisters and brothers, placing all our trust in God's care for us); likewise, only our trust in a spouse's constancy can make possible a radical commitment to a relationship whose theological significance lies in its capacity to represent God's self-giving, forgiving, intimate, constant love for us.

What is the relevance of this criterion for judging whether particular relationships are fittingly blessed by the church's approbation? First, and probably most uncomfortably, the criterion of constancy calls into question the ease with which American churches have made their peace with the phenomenon of remarriage after divorce.[6] Christians ought to manifest more appreciation for the tremendous effort that faithful matrimony requires, more sympathy for the humiliation and frustration and spiritual pain that failed marriages incur, and more critical caution regarding the possibility that projected marriages succeed. While our cultural climate inclines us to keep our noses out of our neighbors' affairs, our role as witnesses to and supporters of a marriage obliges us to speak frankly if we see impediments to the successful sustenance of a marriage. Many who have wrought lengthy marital relationships testify that the effort requires a great deal from the participants and their friends. To the extent that the church recognizes the importance of emphasizing that marriage entails a genuine commitment to mutual constancy, Christians will need to work together to sustain marriages and to sympathetically understand divorce.

Second, the criterion of constancy directs the church's attention away from its habitual scrupulous fascination with genital sexuality. Most Christians are willing to welcome, approve, and ordain lesbian and gay members *so long as* they do not engage in genital sexual relationships—so long as they do not "practice" their sexuality, as if sexual identity were of ethical significance only in moments of genital contact. (Would hand-holding count?) There are countless ways in which human relationships can fall short of God's ideal, and these do not depend on the matter of who does what with whose genitals. Our relationships can be marred by violence committed by one partner against the other. Our relationships can be tainted with a deep current of self-interest, which makes of one's partner simply a commodity for gratifying particular carnal and psychological needs. If we are no longer delighted by our partners, or if we outgrow them, we feel justified in breaking off our relationships with them and seeking out a newer, more satisfying package. Our relationships can be warped by our conviction that each of us should protect a private, individual dimension of our lives for which we are not accountable to those we love. We make commitments with and call for trust from people to whom we are unwilling to entrust our whole selves. All these tendencies debase relations of human intimacy without regard to who is intimate with whom, and the cultural ascendancy of these tendencies makes true, honest, constant commitments all the more difficult to sustain.

Third, the criterion of constancy provides some answers to the questions raised against each of the other proposed approaches. Relations that do not include respect for the criterion of constancy violate God's holiness, for they profess to represent God's steadfast love to the world but instead represent our all-too-human incapacity to fulfill the promises we make. The notion that same-sex couples could manifest godly constancy was alien to the people of ancient Israel, as it is to many today. If we do not rule out such relationships from the beginning of our deliberations, however, we may find that such couples have been abiding in our midst unbeknown to us.

The natural-law argument against homosexual intimacy in Paul has the same status as his natural-law argument against men's having long hair; like the rest of us, Paul repudiates as unnatural that which his culture has excluded as taboo.[7] The list of acts that have been deemed unnatural at one time or another by one or another social group would prohibit practically every form of human endeavor. Indeed, much behavior that lies at the heart of Christian discipleship is profoundly unnatural. Only a naively romantic view would suggest that we are naturally peaceable, gentle, willing to yield, full of mercy and good fruits, without a trace of partiality or hostility. The letter of James identifies these as the effects of a wisdom that comes to us from heaven (3:17), contrasted with the "earthly, unspiritual, devilish" traits of envy, ambition, disorder, and wickedness.

There is no need for defenders of lesbian and gay Christians to appeal to a notion of ecclesiastical rights if we hold up constancy as a criterion of human relationships. Constancy comes in relationships of all kinds, even in intimate sexual relationships against which there are forceful legal, ecclesiastical, and social sanctions. The fact that some gay and lesbian Christians have sustained committed relationships over many years, despite the active opposition that such relationships provoke in many quarters, testifies to an admirable and rare sense of constant fidelity (a constancy that is all the more striking since many partners have undertaken overwhelming responsibilities to nurse their beloved through the devastating effects of AIDS). The dignity and integrity of their discipleship are self-evident.

What then shall we say? Should the church bless committed relationships that bespeak constancy and love when those relationships involve couples of the same sex? In the few passages where scripture addresses the topic directly, it says no. At the same time, the institution of marriage is clearly a human institution, which changes as the Spirit leads us into all truth and as we change our social relations with one another. Whatever else may be true, all participants to the theological discussion of human sexuality should be ready to acknowledge that the institution of marriage has been in constant, gradual change throughout the history of Israel and the church. In Genesis we find polygynous marriages wherein women were valued as objects of exchange; Abraham's servant obtains Rebekah in exchange for jewels, money, and fine garments (Genesis 24), and Jacob exchanges seven years' labor for Leah, then another seven years' labor for Rachel (Genesis 29). The Torah commands that if a husband dies and leaves his wife without a son, his brother-in-law must beget a son for the widow. The "household codes" in New Testament epistles authorize men to exercise domination over their wives. Yet few (if any) churches hold up a model of marriage drawn from Abrahamic or Mosaic texts, and most churches repudiate the male-dominant cast of Pauline marital rhetoric. God's people have amended the institution of marriage as they have discerned elements in it that do not harmonize with other dimensions of Christian life. The mutability of marriage is fitting and good for God's people; as Jesus points out, it is as those who belong to this age that we marry, though marriage is irrelevant with respect to the resurrection life (Luke 20:34). There is no reason inherent in the church's definition of marriage that we should not permit change with respect to same-sex couples when we have allowed change in the marital institution in so many other respects.

Christians therefore must discern whether arguments on behalf of blessing same-sex couples' relationships outweigh the reasons adduced to continue prohibiting such blessings. When familiar arguments about holiness, nature, and rights lead us to an impasse, the criterion of constancy may provide a clear, practical, theologically powerful touchstone for distinguishing intimacies that the church can affirm and support from intimacies that the church must resist. We must deliberate, pray, and examine our consciences, lest prejudice or self-interest predetermine our conclusions. We must seek the mind of Christ to ascertain what best befits God's people. In a word, we need to take seriously precisely the question that my home parish's discussion group shortcircuited.

Why does God care about our sexual lives? Perhaps because the ways that we order our sexual lives signal our highest priorities, our deepest sense of who we are and to whom we can be loyal and true. Some Christians say that couples who have vowed perpetual fidelity, who dedicate their lives to the well-being of their neighbors, who endure exclusion and hardship but who persevere in faith, who forgive those who persecute them and love their enemies, who participate as fully in the life of the church as they are permitted, and who patiently, lovingly embody the covenant of constancy that God has made with us all, ought not to be granted the church's blessing on their mutually trusting relationships. Some might even say that such a commitment is impossible, merely illusory, and that the façade of constancy conceals a rotten structure of depravity. Others—myself included—can only bear witness to what we have heard, what we have seen with our eyes, what we have beheld and touched with our hands—the lives of exemplary discipleship that our sisters and brothers have shared with us. Such lives bring glory to the God of heaven and earth. Such lives are everybody's business, and we are all impoverished if we do not extend to these holy sisters and brothers the church's support for their commitment to constant discipleship.[8]

NOTES

1. The two groups ought not be glibly identified as pro-gay (in the first case) and conservative-traditional (in the second case); some gay Christians hold the second position and experience concomitant destructive self-loathing, while some straight Christians want to reserve the possibility of gratifying their carnal interests apart from theological justifications.
2. James Barr has defended the idea of "natural theology" in the Bible in his Gifford Lectures, published as *Biblical Faith and Natural Theology* (Oxford: Oxford University Press, 1993).
3. If we stipulate that *natural* means "scientifically verifiable," then arguments concerning natural sexuality cannot settle questions by appeal to scripture any more than paleontologists can solve questions about dinosaurs by appealing to Genesis. On the other hand, if we stipulate that *natural* means "according with what we take to be God's will," Paul's assessment of natural sexuality in Romans 1 can no more determine our perspective on what is natural than can his assessment of natural hairstyles in 1 Cor. 11:14 or God's unnatural horticultural practices in Rom. 11:24. Dale Martin has pointed out a number of grave interpretive problems with taking Romans 1 as the last word on natural human sexuality in a paper, "Heterosexism and the Interpretation of Romans 1:26–38," *Biblical Interpretation* 3 (forthcoming).
4. We should be alert to the fact that Old Testament marriage metaphors frequently take a dangerous tack, characterizing God as a spouse who, for a time, abandons Israel to brutal oppression in order to teach Israel a lesson, then returns when Israel has had enough. This is frequently the sort of rhetoric that human spouses parrot to justify spousal abuse, and we would be remiss if we soft-pedaled the damage that such abusive spouses can inflict in the name of God. In the interests of faithfulness to humanity and to God, we need to distinguish codependent abusiveness from genuine fidelity.

5. Katherine Doob Sakenfeld's *Faithfulness in Action* in Overtures to Biblical Theology Series (Philadelphia: Fortress Press, 1985) gives a thorough account of God's *ḥesed* (loyalty; covenant-faithfulness) that greatly enhances the premises of this chapter.

6. No one should use a criterion of constancy as a cruel instrument of coercion to require that people who have fallen into destructive relationships eschew divorce, especially since the church that blessed and promised to support that relationship is implicated in the baneful relationship. If people enter into a marriage that they and their community come to see as unsalvageable, they should acknowledge that state of affairs and bring the relationship to an end. In such a case, not only the ex-spouses have failed; the congregation that gathered to witness the marriage and that committed itself to do all in its power to uphold them in their marriage also shares the failure. The church should thus penitently recognize and compassionately share the pain that comes with acknowledging such an error in judgment and should promptly act to embody God's reconciling love to divorced sisters and brothers. The church should not, however, take lightly this sign that the participants in the (former) marriage proved unable to live out the commitments they had made, and should be extremely cautious about supposing that the divorced parties have attained sufficient perspective on that misunderstanding to undertake again the commitments that inhere in the vocation of Christian marriage. (And the clergy and congregation should undertake careful self-examination to ascertain how they might have prevented such a regrettable end to the joyous beginning of the marriage.)

7. Once again, Dale Martin makes a case that the term *natural*, in first-century ethical discourse, is perhaps best interpreted as *conventional* in "Heterosexism and the Interpretation of Romans 1:26–38," in which he cites illuminating examples from the Hellenistic literature.

8. I must convey my thanks to Juliet Richardson and to Philip Kenneson for their very helpful criticisms of an earlier draft of this chapter.

I consider it a privilege to present this chapter as a partial sign of my gratitude to my lesbian and gay sisters and brothers, who have taught me much about constancy, about patient endurance, about following a path of self-giving love, and about the costs of truth.

12

The Heterosexual Norm

Max L. Stackhouse

Christians are heirs to biblically based traditions that are reasonable, coherent, valid for all, and pertinent to public policy as well as to personal behavior. These traditions hold, among other things, that heterosexual marriage is the norm for the exercise of human sexuality. This view recently has come under attack in our society and in parts of the church by a movement that claims the "co-equal" moral status of the sexual orientations, choices, or actions of persons who consider themselves gay, lesbian, or bisexual. This movement seeks not only acknowledgement; it seeks affirmation. It wants not only an acceptance of the fact that some people experience themselves as different from the traditional norm; it wants this experience to be socially, legally, morally, and spiritually approved. It not only urges that alternative sexual dispositions and behaviors be free from harassment and punishment when they occur in private; it demands that they be acknowledged as ethical and theologically legitimate.

Such demands have left many who are not personally hostile to difference—but are concerned with supporting what is right and good and not idealizing anything less—uncertain as to how to debate the issues. Since the movement has generated a vocabulary by which it assaults any who do not agree to the agenda it advocates, debate is difficult. The unconvinced are often accused of bigotry, ignorance, repressive authoritarianism, sexual chauvinism ("heterosexism"), or psychological pathology ("homophobia"), as if any moral reservations on this question could only be rooted in an immoral unwillingness to face the facts, a desire to dominate, a lust for power, or some other irrational prejudice.

Thus, many have fallen silent on this question, reluctant to discuss homosexuality, to affirm their deepest convictions about it, or even to discuss openly and honestly the relative merits of the arguments. Those who are not silent risk the vilification that comes from those who consider themselves open and affirming.

It is certainly true that some who call themselves Christian have confused the tradition they confess with ideas that derive from prudish denials of sexuality as a gift of God, culturally established gender roles, arrogant self-righteousness, or psychosocial pathologies. Some believers have been hateful to their neighbors in the name of religion. Some versions of the faith have been repressive of wholesome sexual impulses and have wrongly condemned other people to second-class citizenship. These betrayals of Christianity deserve severe condemnation—not only because they have broken faith with the tradition in the name of the faith but also because they unlovingly distort what is true about the human condition.

In the face of both the challenges to and betrayals of the tradition, one of the most caring ways to proceed may be to restate the case for the classical tradition and tell why it remains basically valid, and to show why the opposing views ought not to be followed. Moreover, since these religious traditions have been a formative influence in the history of law, what we examine and reaffirm is pertinent not only to our heritage but to the moral fabric of the common life.

Christians claim that all persons are made in the image of God, and this view has gradually been recognized by many to imply that people ought not to be abused, oppressed, victimized, tortured, or tormented. The dignity of each person, even those whose behavior is morally repugnant to some, is to be respected by individuals and protected by law. Indeed, we are to love our neighbors, and one way to do this is to make sure that common human rights are available to all. There is no justification for the violent viciousness sometimes shown by sexually insecure and homophobic people against those who are identified as gay, and it can and should be constrained by civil authority as well as by religious and social condemnation.

The acknowledgment of human rights and the granting of due respect do not, however, require the conclusion that all opinions are of equal importance, that all lifestyles must be equally honored, or that all behaviors should go equally unchallenged. It is also a mark of respect to take others' ideas seriously enough to dispute or refute them openly—especially when one thinks they are fundamentally mistaken or are leading individuals, communities, or societies in destructive directions.

A second and related theme arising from our tradition is the idea that government is not to control all areas of life. Religious beliefs, practices, and groups have rights to exist that cannot be denied by the state. This limitation on the state demands the recognition that areas of moral, convictional, emotional, and spiritual life must remain outside the jurisdiction of government. Not all sins are crimes. Beliefs and practices that may properly be demanded by a faith community need not be, and in some cases may not be, required by any state, just as some behaviors that evoke demands for repentance in a faith community must be permitted by the state. In areas that touch on the dispositions of the heart, the state is not competent and the law is an improper instrument of control, just as many personal opinions, inclinations, associations, and loyalties may not disqualify a person from citizenship or from the exercise of civil liberties or duties.

A third pertinent teaching of our heritage is the moral and spiritual equality of the races and of males and females. To be sure, only parts of the tradition have participated in efforts to reach a degree of social, political, and economic equity with regard to race and gender. However, those streams of the tradition have more rightly understood the deeper presuppositions and implication of both the biblical heritage and the basic constituting structure of human life than they have the alternatives. The overcoming of racism and sexism remains a priority for religious bodies and social policy.

But just as some cannot distinguish between sin and crime, others can see no distinction between homosexuals as a minority group and other groups that have been the victims of discrimination—specifically African Americans and women. In some ways, they would seem to have a good argument. Insofar as social stereotypes or prejudices disqualify some people from fulfilling their callings and using their gifts to serve God and the neighbor, the state has a positive obligation to prevent unjustly imposed disadvantages.

However, in two ways the argument is doubtful. First, there is no element of personal choice that determines sex or race in any who are female or black (or male or white). Thus, any suggestion of a moral or spiritual quality intrinsic to these conditions is theological nonsense. Indeed, we often properly judge ourselves and each other when too much fervor is invested in this or that cultural definition of gender or ethnic roles.

Second, no specific set of moral behaviors can be attributed to anyone who is female or black (or Asian or Hispanic) when sex or race is lived out, and it is sexist or racist to insist that it can. Moral choices can be made in regard to how we embrace or resist, channel or live out biophysical and social-psychological promptings. In respect to neither sex nor race can it be said that will or identity is dependent on a pre-given disposition that must not only be expressed but approved by church and society in order to realize personhood. In this connection, the nineteenth-century theory that homosexuality is a medical and social "third sex," beyond the reach of theology and ethics, is very doubtful.

There may indeed be better reasons to reassert the importance of the ethical norm of heterosexuality in intimate relationships. The biblical and theological traditions reveal to us aspects of the human condition that are reasonable, in accord with the depths of human experience, and valid for all peoples in spite of the fact that the Fall tempts us to deny not only revelation but the depths of experience and reason that it both grounds and confirms.

First, and at the most basic level, homosexuality is contrary to the intentions of creation. The structure of sex organs is such that one of their purposes is human reproduction. That is not the only purpose, but it is a real and an undeniable purpose—and it is a purpose not capable of being fulfilled homosexually. It is not wrong in this regard, thus, to speak of homosexuality as a terminal sexual behavior. It cannot transmit the gift of life to the next generation. This is not the only terminal sexual condition, but the fact remains that it is one, and thus an undeniable tragedy. Like other difficulties of infertility, it may properly be lamented even if, out of necessity, the difficulties are accepted.

For another, ours is a world greatly concerned about nature in terms of ecology but reluctant to speak of "human nature"—as if humanity had no constitution. This is so because some understand nature to be only material existence and take nature in this sense to be the ultimate court of appeal in all things. Recent, if still debated, biological evidence about differences in the development of the brain provides some people with the evidence that sexual orientation is genetically determined. They immediately infer that sexual orientation is beyond any evaluation that implies rightness or wrongness, good or evil, better or worse.

Frequently, however, those who take a materialist view of nature are morally selective—and even sometimes unreflective—when it comes to the use of technology. Many biological differences exist, and we constantly make judgments as to whether corrective action should be taken—surgical, endocrinological, physical or psycho-therapeutic. Many wear glasses or braces, struggle with diet and exercise, take regular medication, or undergo regimens of therapy in order to live rightly and well; and we often believe those who do not do so to be irresponsible.

If homosexuality is genetically determined and if we do (or could) develop the capacity to alter this condition by genetic engineering (or therapy), the ethical question is whether we should do so. In other words, the moral question is not settled; it is merely relocated. The very existence of genetic engineering and multiple therapies suggests that a great number of things that are natural are also held to be non-normative and morally alterable. Issues of the will and of morality do not therefore cease to exist. Naturalistic data cannot tell us whether nature can or should be genetically altered, or whether parents may seek and doctors be allowed to alter the genetic makeup of, say, a fetus with a propensity to homosexuality.

It would be odd indeed if biological factors had nothing to do with sexual drives, but genetics (and biology in general) alone is not determinative of the human personality or of all that must be acknowledged as moral or immoral in regard to sexuality. Humans are creatures of spirit and of society, as well as of genetics and nutrition; it is a dehumanizing view to deny them moral agency in their human relations. Even if we have only limited capacities to modify inherited tendencies, personal habits and social policies can reduce the frequency and effects of conditions that constrict life—as we have seen with alcohol abuse, learning disabilities, heart trouble, and other conditions. The issues remain: How should we use the will we have?

Others recognize this, but then argue that sexual orientation is basically constructed through social conditions. They say that homosexuality is a result of the way people are raised or of the opportunities for affection that come to persons in the course of development. Some, indeed, extend this idea and argue that the cultural channels of identity carved out by society for people with various self-images, needs, or potentialities is what shapes our orientations. In these views, we are thrust into sexual roles that are artifacts of history, often shaped by the will of the powerful to dominate the weak. Since we know this, they say, we ought to take responsibility for how we shape the society to protect the weak. In this view, we have to recognize that some people are determined by their social circumstances to experience themselves one way or another, and we have to adapt the laws, customs, and mores of society to their reality so that they are no longer victims.

Again, it would be strange indeed if the way one is treated as a child, the models one observes in the home, or the wider culture did not influence sexual self-definition. Surely, the very unique way in which each individual experiences the possibilities of love shapes sexual identity to a substantial degree. Not only are we all socialized or acculturated into definitions of identity, some people undoubtedly feel that they cannot fit into the images of male or female presented to them. Some feel the anguish of "being different" and adopt alternative or marginalized definitions of self.

What is not at all clear in this view, however, is why we should accept the socially constructed stereotypes that exaggerate sexual characteristics in artificial ways and wound people in the first place. If they are socially constructed, they can surely be reconstructed by the reform of laws, customs, mores, and religious teachings. But why should they be reconstructed in the directions gay/lesbian/bisexual movements advocate? Why should the victims of a damaging social construction become the standard for the reconstruction? And why shouldn't we intentionally alter the patterns of childrearing and the images of identity that drive people into the anguished feelings of difference, and thus encourage a percentage of the population to turn to homosexual lifestyles—or for that matter, that encourage some heterosexuals to adopt such exaggerated images of masculinity or femininity that anorexia among young women and steroids among young men become serious problems?

The best available crosscultural evidence suggests that channels of sexual identity are somewhat malleable. They can be at least partially constructed, deconstructed, or reconstructed—although with great difficulty and over long periods of time. In fact, the evidence suggests that a variety of sexual models have been and can be developed and that homosexuality is itself a social construction subject to various degrees of deconstruction and reconstruction. One of the problems of the theory of social construction is that it gives us no sense of a guiding norm about what ought to be constructed or reconstructed, and it thus leaves us in a situation of presumptive values or power politics without well-grounded theological or ethical standards.

Neither side of the ancient nature-or-nurture argument has won the day. Both sides have partially valid insights, but neither one touches the deeper levels of human nature, and neither surpasses or refutes the truth and wisdom of the classic theological view. In fact, human nature is neither a simple biological function nor a social artifact, nor a dialectic of the two. The inclination felt to orient one's love life in one direction or another grows out of some combination of these two factors, *plus* several others that are seldom discussed in many current debates. Besides, the presence of an inclination from these two factors does not tell us how to exercise the will, although the reality of the will appears in every technological intervention in nature and in every attempt to reconstruct the social patterns of life. The inevitable necessity of dealing with the will, and thus with a normative model to guide the will, brings us to issues that are, once again, inevitably ethical and ultimately theological.

Recognition of the fact that humans are not simply creatures driven by nature and nurture but are creatures having a will has led other partisans in these debates to assert the sovereignty of freedom. Sometimes in libertarian and sometimes in liberationist terms, it is just presumed these days that people are obviously not *simply* driven by natural impulses or social conditions. People inevitably exercise a substantial measure of freedom over how they will live their sexual lives, and that is how it should be. Is it not so that the highest value is freedom? that each person must be free to decide how to live his or her life as he or she wishes? and that no one has a right to impose any values on that freedom?

Many intentional and more unintentional heirs of Romantic, existential, and postmodern philosophies of freedom fear anything that approaches "essentialism," for essentialism—whether that essence is ontological, theological, or ethical—would compromise the absoluteness of the freedom they desire to have and they think humans should have. There is confusion in this argument, however. To hold this position, one must believe that the essence of human nature is free will. This view makes each person responsible for the exercise of choice, but gives no guidance as to what choices might be responsible or desirable. Thus, if some people decide, for whatever reason, to deny support or approval to those who do not limit their sexual freedom, those who hold this view may freely disagree and pursue their own free lifestyles, but they have no moral grounds to prevent the rest of the population from freely refusing to employ, support, house, medically treat, or otherwise protect their lifestyles.

The implications of this view turn out to be devastating. It can provide neither constraints against evils nor positive guides to the good in common life. The skeptics doubt any essentialism—the view that there is a fixed aspect of human existence to which all are subject regardless of biological influences, social conditioning, or free choices. If there is a universal reality to which all must submit, the liberty of humans to arbitrarily construct the world with technology, social change advocacy, and the assertion of unfettered freedom, is in error. The suspicion of essentialism is based on a desire for the freedom to create and recreate the world according to our own imaginations. But a world in which our essential nature is simply a freedom to create things as we imagine and to cultivate the power to do so is a world in which the imaginative and the powerful will completely dominate all things all the more. Such a world is ultimately far more dangerous and threatening—even to freedom itself—than one in which we seek a truth to which all must equally submit.

In contrast to these views, the classical Christian view offers a truth that is more consistent and accurate to the human condition, one that can and should be persuasive to all people, and to which all people ought to submit equally. To present a normative standard for human behavior is no threat to humanity, nor is it inconsistent with natural or social influences or human freedom. Human beings are both *finite*—made, as Genesis puts it, from the dust of the ground, and *free*—made with the capacity to cultivate the earth, name the animals, relate to one another, and respond to God. We are, thus, both rooted in the concrete limitations of physicality, social location, and need, and always able, in some indeterminate degree, to transcend precisely these limitations. The essence of human nature is that we have a complex character. We are in turn material, relational, and spiritual; we are less than angels, but more than beasts; we are products of our societies, but makers of civilizations; we are driven by passions, but we also choose whom to love and how to enact that love; we make real choices, but we know that we ought to choose rightly and well.

Because we are such creatures, the form that our loves should take is not determined by biological definitions of the natural, by the conditioned roles that have become "second nature" in our social contexts, or by unencumbered, arbitrary choices. All play a role, but it is our nature (in this deeper, broader understanding of the term) to reshape our biophysical nature and our cultural "second nature," by the use of our freedom, and to do so under limits that are not made by us, but given in the kinds of creatures we are. And because we are not only free but finite, we find ways of indulging our physical existence that are destructive of our biophysical possibilities, ways of building our relationships in society that destroy our sociocultural contexts, and ways of exercising our wills that undercut even our capacities to enhance freedom.

The morally normative, therefore, is that which is appropriate to the sort of creatures we are—physical, social, and willing beings in relationship to God, made for just relationships between persons that sustain and enhance life over time. Therefore, love (specifically sexual love) should have a form suited to that norm, a form already present in the normative teachings of our traditions because that tradition touches the very core of what we really are.

All humans are created in God's image, and each is also created, secondarily, as male or female—neither of which can be both or the other without a distortion of our nature. All are bound together in communities of love and duty, under God, in religious communities of faith and in civil communities of justice when those communities recognize the God-given dignity of each. When our sexuality is actualized in its distinctive way, it is understood to be a call for faithfulness to our male or our female humanness in the context of the whole web of life—biophysical, social, moral, and religious. It is thus a call to that kind of responsive and responsible relationship in which we together take up the task of being male and female in our sexual relationship. It is a call to forge a true community between those whose sexuality is complementary, mutually enhancing, and life-giving. Faithful, enduring, fertile marriage bonds are a paradigmatic form of life.

The bond of marriage has a threefold significance: It is, first, a procreative bond, as mentioned above. Not every marriage is blessed with children, and for those so blessed, childbearing is only a part of the couple's married life. Yet providing a stable, wholesome context for the nurture of the next generation, one that itself is capable of providing the context for the generation after that, occupies a large share of a childbearing couple's time, energy, and commitment. This does not end when children are grown. Still, the differentiation of male and female is ordered toward the possibility of offspring, toward the perpetuation of the species. This is a key means by which God sustains human life and provides the context of nurture—both of which allow the larger purposes of all creation to be fulfilled.

This blessing is, however, also a responsibility that we ought not choose to avoid. It is the task of sharing in the creativity of God, playing our parts under God's guidance as co-creators, committing ourselves to the ongoing life, specifically the life of people seeking to be faithful to the covenants of God. The acceptance of the call indicates a task undertaken in faith and with a hope for meanings that far transcend our individual desires and felt needs. To turn deliberately away from this call, except to undertake another one that also fulfills God's purposes and draws one into a community that extends over generations, or to order the common life so that many find it advantageous to reject this call, distorts our creaturehood and misses a truth that ought to become actualized in our life. In God's good providence, we give birth to and nurture those who will succeed us. We generate and support with joy and care, we wither and perish so that others may flourish.

Second, the marriage bond is a community of love between those who are "other." This means not simply "an-other" person, but one who is truly "other" even, and especially including, both the body, its characteristics, and the social roles and expectations to which males and females are differently exposed. The bond of marriage is not, therefore, understood to be primarily a means of individual fulfillment. It is a doubtful view that each one must "get his or her sexual identity straight" and then seek the appropriate kind of liaison to meet that individual need, especially since individual senses of sexual identity can be falsely framed by biophysical distortions, social constructions, or irresponsible uses of freedom. Christians understand that we require the "other" to be whole in areas of sexuality. Sexual identity is relational from the start. To be sure, marriage affords an answer to human loneliness. Some remain lonely because they do not find a suitable spouse. Some remain lonely in what looks like a marriage. These are tragedies with which many wrestle. Some overcome loneliness in nonsexual relationships between males and females or between same-sexed persons. These relations should not be condemned; nor can we judge harshly those who, to avoid loneliness and temptations to random relationships, quietly establish enduring, loving, same-sexed partnerships.

In all cases, communities of faith who know that God is in relationship to each and that no one is ultimately alone need to establish contexts in which loneliness is reduced. Further, all people in these conditions should be encouraged to reach out through community organizations, personal charities, and through tax policy to those who are not like themselves and to assume concrete forms of responsibility for coming generations.

The marriage of a man to a woman, however, remains the normative physical, social, and moral sign that we are not meant to be isolated individuals or to focus only on relationships with those who are already much like us. We are created for community with the Divine Other and with the human other, and the bonding of sexual otherness is the immediate and obvious evidence of this. The relative integrity of various alternatives under certain conditions does not relativize the normative character of these relationships.

Third, the family is a decisive building block in society, a fact that has several dimensions. Every civilization needs certain institutions to exist; no society can flourish without an economy, a political order, a language by which to communicate, a family system, and, above all, a religion. Such *orders*, as they are sometimes called, are not only the functional requirements of human social existence but the interlocked structures by which our human propensities to egoism, selfishness, shortsightedness, and carelessness

are constrained and the possibilities of altruism, generosity, long-range vision, and engagement are evoked. These call us to contribute to the whole
of life by making us concretely involved in forming a loving, just, and sus-
tainable society that anticipates the New Jerusalem for which we hope.

The family, while it inevitably involves a division of labor and a structure of authority (as, for example, between parents and children), best flour-
ishes when it also is governed by principles that recognize the rights and
needs of each member, measures out duties and responsibilities with equity,
rewards and punishments with compassion, and constantly schools all
members in the necessity of mutuality, responsiveness, and duty to the
commonwealth. Those who have no fundamental stake in the networks and
institutions that sustain the whole society and reach toward the long future
may be quite concerned about one or several orders of society, and their
concern and involvement should be honored. But their condition does not
necessitate sustained commitment and their daily lives do not require the
constant forming of others to have regard for these structures of civility.

More personally, marriage is a *healing* bond in which the sinful impulses,
tendencies, and pathologies present in all are disciplined, restrained, and
repaired, and in which—with God's help—we pursue a path toward holiness, the true pattern of wholeness. In marriage, we begin to learn the
meaning and difficulty of committed love, in sickness and in health, for better or for worse, for richer or for poorer. We pledge fidelity to the spouse
as we make ourselves physically, socially, emotionally, and spiritually vul-
nerable to and before each other. This revealing and giving of the self calls
for faithfulness in response, and it demands trust, forgiveness, and acceptance on the parts of both partners.

A good measure of healing and wholeness can be found elsewhere than
in marriage, most notably in communities of faith, but also in many close
companionships, in various support groups, and in some stable, caring,
same-sex relationships. Even if they be assessed as less than complete in one
or another way, it would be wrong to prevent anyone by force of law from
attempting to live out the most complete healing community possible.
Wherever the possibilities of healing occur, fidelity, trust, forgiveness, mutual edification, and acceptance are both necessary ethical principles and
means for that healing. Casual, promiscuous, exploitative, or commercial
sex is a turning away from the healing that the community of faith, and the
marriage bond with regard to sexuality, is intended to bring.

It is a mistake to infer, however, that all forms of healing relationship are
equally ideal and should be equally invested with the same moral, social,
and spiritual legitimacy. Certain key elements of our traditions know that
the very ecstasy of sexuality, its sheer delights and pleasures, take us out of
ourselves and make alive in our bodies a consciousness of the mystery of
another realm of being. In some traditions, sexual images and familial

symbols have been used to convey dimensions of transcendence that cannot easily be conveyed otherwise. Love has also inspired much of the great poetry, music, art, and literature by which humans communicate the more subtle emotions.

The proper form of gratitude for these gracious gifts is not to embrace every occasion where that ecstasy may occur, but to develop—in the arts, in the art of lovemaking, and in the covenants of mutual responsibility in which they occur—the most holy embodiments of these mysteries that we can find. We offer, in other words, the best that humanity can offer to the source from which our humanity comes. Even as we acknowledge its relative inadequacy, we seek to conform it to the highest, widest, deepest, broadest model available to humanity.

These things we learn from scripture, from our traditions, from reason, and from an examination of the best evidence we can find, and this we commend to all: The current confusions are widespread, and many of them are based in ideas or commitments that are incomplete or inconsistent at best; distorted and ideological at worst. In contrast, Christian ideas of heterosexual marriage more accurately grasp and guide human condition and understand the promise and perils of human sexuality. In heterosexual marriage, we confront the fact of our mortality and the possibility of concretely participating with God in the hope of life beyond death, trusting in God to preserve human life and fulfill the purposes of creation. In it, we confront the true meanings of difference and find the clue to the forming of genuine communities of difference and structures indispensable to the well-being of souls and civilizations.

The Christian traditions more accurately grasp and support the norm that reflects the best we can know of God's law and purposes, and that allows life and love to flourish, than both the movements that seek to transform that heritage or the reactionaries who confuse them with constricted prudery.

13

How to Discuss Moral Issues Surrounding Homosexuality When You Know You Are Right

Nancy J. Duff

When There Is No Moral Dilemma

A moral dilemma exists either when one discovers equally plausible (but mutually exclusive) alternatives to a moral issue or when one finds no adequate solution at all to an issue. When people encounter a moral dilemma, they are more inclined to listen to opposing points of view than they are when they know with certainty that their position is the morally correct one. Some moral issues do not represent dilemmas for some people.[1] Such was the case, for instance, in the fight against segregated schools. For the civil rights workers, no moral dilemma existed in the question of whether public schools should be integrated. The arguments of the segregationists simply held no moral weight.

Abortion provides an example of a moral issue that some experience as a dilemma and others do not. Some people hear both pro-choice and pro-life arguments as equally compelling; hence, abortion presents them with an agonizing dilemma. Staunch pro-choice and pro-life advocates, however, discover no moral dilemma in the issue. The one finds a woman's right to determine what happens to her body a self-evident freedom; the other finds the fetus's status as a human being and its right to live equally self-evident. No moral dilemma exists for these pro-choice and pro-life advocates. The person who finds in abortion an agonizing dilemma will listen intently to both sides of the argument; the person who finds in abortion no moral dilemma is not likely to listen to the opposing point of view at all. Hence, we have the stalemate that presently exists wherein each side talks (or screams) past the other.

A similar situation exists within the church in the argument over homosexuality. Some Christians find that the issues surrounding homosexuality represent a true moral dilemma; they hear equally valid but conflicting arguments regarding biblical and theological interpretations, ordination, same-sex unions, gay and lesbian parenting, and other issues. Whereas these Christians are likely to listen intently to different arguments, those members of the church who find no moral dilemma in the issues will tend to argue their own position vehemently but listen very little to the opposing points of view.

For Christians who uphold the ordination of homosexuals and the appropriateness of church-sanctioned homosexual unions, the opposing arguments are parallel to those of racists; such arguments cannot be given the honor of a fair hearing because they are themselves so prejudicial. For Christians who reject the ordination of homosexuals and the appropriateness of church-sanctioned homosexual unions, the opposing arguments are the products of a society and of a church that have lost their moral grounding; the arguments cannot be given the honor of a fair hearing because they are base and baseless, running counter to divine revelation. Although both sides continue to present their arguments, hoping to persuade those who have not already made up their minds, more energy is often given to strategies for winning the political day than to discussing the issue with opponents. As a result, the church is torn between two equally committed factions, each believing that it has taken the moral high road, each believing that it represents the will of God, and each seeking to win.

I myself stand among those who encounter no moral dilemma in the issues surrounding homosexuality. Like many people with firm convictions on the issues, I too find it difficult to listen to views that oppose my own because I believe the position I hold is so obviously the right one. I stand with those who uphold the ordination of homosexuals, who believe that faithful, monogamous relationships among lesbians and gay men can be consistent with the will of God, that gays and lesbians can be responsible parents, that their commitment to lifelong, monogamous union should be recognized as parallel to marriage, and that their right to adopt children should be upheld. These issues do not, for me, present a moral dilemma, that is, I do not see two equally plausible but mutually exclusive alternatives to these issues; nor do I interpret them as problems for which no adequate solutions exist. Furthermore, I firmly believe that the Gospel provides the basis for my point of view.

I know that many Christians who hold the opposing point of view feel as strongly about their position as I do about mine. They find it difficult to listen to views that oppose their own because they believe the position they hold is so obviously the right one. They stand against the ordination of homosexuals, believe that sexual relationships among lesbians and gay men cannot be consistent with the will of God, that gays and lesbians cannot be responsible parents, that gay and lesbian unions should not be recognized as parallel to marriage, and that gays and lesbians have no right to adopt children. These issues do not, for them, present a moral dilemma. They do not see two equally plausible but mutually exclusive alternatives to these issues; nor do they interpret them as problems for which no adequate solutions exist. Furthermore, they firmly believe that the Gospel provides the basis for their point of view.

This absence of any sense of moral dilemma (found on both sides of the issue) coupled with the certainty of being morally consistent with the will of God fuels the already strong emotions that arise in the debate over issues surrounding homosexuality. As a theologian who has chosen to focus her teaching and scholarship primarily on theological ethics, I find myself weary of the argument raging over homosexuality in the church. I would much rather focus my attention on the doctrine of vocation, issues in medical ethics, or issues involving children than to jump into the fray of this current battle. I would much rather see the church address issues of poverty and violence then spend its energy arguing *this* issue. I would rather ignore my opponents, stand with my allies, support gays and lesbians in ways that I can, and turn my attention to other matters.

There *is*, however, a battle raging over the issue of sexual orientation in the church to which I belong and in the world in which I live. Although many of us would not choose *this* as the issue to occupy our attention, it has presented itself to us. The battle will rage on even if we choose to ignore it. Faithful responsibility demands that one address the issues given to us. One feels compelled to ask, however, whether it is possible to discuss an issue responsibly with opponents when convinced that the position one holds is the morally correct one. Because neither side in this debate can recognize truth in the other's position, each side is tempted to disregard the value of both the debate and the opponent and simply seek to win, no matter what the cost to the church.

I have discovered that a rather unlikely source—a nineteenth-century secular philosopher—helps convince me not to turn away from the debate altogether and not to attempt to win the political fight with callous disregard for my opponents. In his essay "On Liberty," John Stuart Mill gives three reasons why we should listen to opposing points of view, even when we know that our position is the correct one.[2]

First, Mill challenges us to admit that *because we are fallible, if we silence an opposing opinion we may indeed be silencing the truth.*[3] Given that we are fallible, Mill takes comfort in the possibility of rectifying our mistakes through discussion and experience. This point, of course, is the one least likely to speak to people on opposing sides of the issues surrounding homosexuality. Though we may know we are fallible in general, we do not believe we are mistaken on *this* issue. Nevertheless, Mill rightly claims that a significant distinction exists between the assumption that an opinion is true because it has withstood opposition and assuming it is true in order to stifle opposition.[4]

Second, Mills points out that even if the opposing opinion is clearly in error, *it may contain a portion of the truth.*[5] It is only by the collision of adverse opinions that the remainder of the truth has any chance of being supplied. Here we have more reason to listen to Mill. When both sides refuse to listen to each other, neither has the opportunity to listen to that portion of the truth that the other may hold. As a result, two opportunities are lost. Each side loses the opportunity to correct something that may be wrong about a particular point of its own argument. Furthermore, each side loses the opportunity to persuade its opponent by acknowledging what is true about the opponent's position and then supplying the remainder of the truth.

Finally, Mill contends that even if the opinion we hold is not only true, but represents the whole truth, *it risks becoming no more than prejudice or recitation if it refuses to be in conversation with other opinions.*[6] Mill believes that we strengthen our own position by listening to arguments against it, rightly claiming that the one whose judgment can be trusted is the one who has listened to a variety of opposing positions.[7]

The church today would do well to listen to Mill's argument. He is neither claiming that all points of view are equally valid nor suggesting that one should abandon the conviction of one's position. He is suggesting, however, that even out of a position of great conviction, listening to one's opponents is necessary. I believe that his claims coincide with the Gospel. Although there are isolated times when scriptures counsel us to throw out an offender, we are taught by the Gospel to disagree in love. It seems to me that those of us who stand on opposite sides of this issue are now on the brink of throwing each other out of the church or of bailing out ourselves. We are so disturbed by the idea that the other side could win the day that we find it hard to recognize each other as truly Christian.

In any debate as highly charged as the one over homosexuality, there are always some people on both sides who become so extreme in their approach to debate, so willing to resort to malicious and dishonest tactics, that it is simply impossible and even irresponsible to listen to their position. I am not suggesting that people who fall into this category—whatever side of the debate they represent—should be given a fair hearing by their opponents. I am, rather, urging both sides of the issue to avoid these errors by disagreeing with each other in the spirit of Christian love, acknowledging readily any truth held by their opponent, and being mindful that people on both sides of the debate stand under both the judgment and the grace of God.

Debating Homosexuality: Looking for Truth in the Opponent's Position

In the summer of 1993 at a highly charged General Assembly, the Presbyterian Church (U.S.A.) voted to uphold and even strengthen its previous stance against the ordination of homosexuals, but it also agreed to enter a three-year study of the issue.[8] Since then, we have heard both responsible and irresponsible claims, counterclaims, debate, and reporting on both sides of the issue by various members and groups within the Presbyterian Church (U.S.A.). The institution where I work, Princeton Theological Seminary, has experienced both constructive and destructive debate over the issue. Faculty, students, administration, and staff who either support or oppose the ordination of homosexuals have been angry, hurt, and disillusioned by the contentions and actions of their opponents. Many of us on both sides of the issue, however, have also experienced genuine encounters, mutual enrichment, and reconciliation with one another even in the midst of strong disagreement. Furthermore, no matter what our experience, we all fear the divisive effects this debate and its outcome will have on the church.

A month before General Assembly met in 1993, a document was generated by some members of the Princeton Seminary community. Titled "A Princeton Declaration," it spoke against the ordination of "individuals engaged in homosexual practice."[9] The document generated an immediate reaction at the Seminary and eventually throughout the Presbyterian Church. Some members of the faculty at Princeton Seminary (myself included) generated "A Counter Declaration" that disagreed with both the content of "A Princeton Declaration" and the process by which it was produced. The ensuing debate over both documents was highly charged, divisive, and often hurtful.

During the following academic year, however, the Seminary sponsored several events that encouraged and modeled responsible discussion of the issues surrounding homosexuality. Many people on both sides of the issue expressed their appreciation for these discussions and, in some cases, opponents discovered some ground for mutual respect even in light of profound disagreement. As hurtful as many of us believed "A Princeton Declaration" to be when it was first presented, I credit those who generated the document with initiating a series of events that brought the issues surrounding homosexuality to open discussion on campus.

In the pages that follow, I intend to present and respond to the position of those who oppose both the ordination of homosexuals and the church's affirmation of monogamous homosexual unions. I have chosen to confine most of my comments to "A Princeton Declaration." Although it is my intention to refute the arguments of my opponents, one of my primary aims is to demonstrate what I believe is true about their position and what we all can learn from it. As a result, I hope that my argument will be heard as one respectful of my opponents and that I will readily admit weaknesses in the arguments of some of my allies.

In order to address the arguments offered in "A Princeton Declaration," I will describe and respond to four objections presented by the document against various issues regarding homosexuality. The identification of these as "objections" and their numbering are my own. Each objection, however,

will be set forth as a direct quotation from the document. In this way I hope
to let the arguments of "A Princeton Declaration" speak for themselves.

> *Objection 1:* The term "homophobic" is often carelessly applied to anyone
> who expresses a strong dislike for homosexual behavior. But those of us
> who consider the practice of homosexuality wrong from a biblical and
> moral standpoint, who do not believe that it is a legitimate or healthy
> Christian lifestyle, and who oppose the ordination of people who prac-
> tice it, are not necessarily homophobic. We oppose fornication, but are
> not afraid of fornicators. We oppose adultery, but are not afraid of adul-
> terers. We oppose homosexuality, but are not afraid of homosexuals.

Two significant terms in this objection merit our attention: *homophobic*
and *lifestyle*. The Declaration correctly points out that those who oppose
the ordination of homosexuals are not *necessarily* homophobic. People who
stand on both sides of this issue have something to learn from this claim.
On the one hand, those who support the ordination of homosexuals need
to acknowledge that the term *homophobic* cannot be used against everyone
who stands opposed to homosexual behavior. The automatic charge of homophobia at the first hint that someone deems homosexual activity to be a
sin cuts off conversation and caricatures the position of one's opponent.
Some people stand opposed to homosexual activity not because they are homophobic but because they are led to such a position by their interpretation of the Bible and their commitment to the Gospel.

On the other hand, people who oppose the ordination of homosexuals
need to acknowledge that some people who speak against homosexuality
exhibit homophobic tendencies.[10] Homophobia can be recognized in situations where one protests homosexual activity by engaging in acts of cruelty that are more serious than the "sin" being protested.[11] Homophobia
also exists in situations where one who has been a strong opponent of homosexual activity is discovered to be homosexual.[12] Such people may believe that their sexual feelings are wrong and that making strong public
statements against homosexuality is one way to counter and change their
own feelings. Their stand against homosexuality grows in part out of
hypocrisy, confusion, and fear of what they may discover in themselves.

Admitting that homophobia does exist, however, in no way suggests that
all people who speak against homosexuality are either cruel, hypocritical,
or struggling with their own sexual identity. It does, however, allow those
who oppose homosexual activity to be realistic about some people who
agree with them. In fact, Christians on both sides of the issue should be
leery of the arguments and actions of some of their allies. No one has to
hold in high esteem all who agree with them.

Homophobia is not a useless word, but perhaps it is an overly used one.
People who reject arguments for the moral integrity of homosexual activity can admit that homophobia exists without undermining their position.

In fact, they strengthen their position by setting themselves against those who argue from a position of hypocrisy, confusion, or cruelty. People who support arguments for the moral integrity of homosexual activity need to recognize that the charge of homophobia does not fit all their opponents and should, therefore, be reserved only for those whose position is clearly hypocritical or unusually cruel.

"Lifestyle" represents another term found in "Objection 1" that requires some clarification. The writers of "A Princeton Declaration" claim that homosexuality is not a "legitimate or healthy Christian lifestyle." While the intention here is a good one (to condemn homosexual activity without demonizing the homosexual person), *lifestyle* is an imprecise term. Those who agree with "A Princeton Declaration" are not protesting a particular lifestyle, but rather all homosexual behavior, that is, all intimate, sexual behavior between two people of the same sex. The morality of this behavior is rejected whether it occurs in the context of a monogamous relationship or in the context of frequent, multiple sex partners.

Those who support the morality of certain types of homosexual behavior, however, will eschew the use of *lifestyle* to describe all homosexuals. Homosexuals, like heterosexuals, engage in a variety of lifestyles; some choose to be involved in lifelong, monogamous relationships, while others may be involved in multiple sexual encounters throughout their lives. Whereas some people may support the morality of any kind of sexual behavior between consenting adults, others make distinctions regarding the context, intentions, and commitments of the adults engaged in sexual behavior—whether homosexual or heterosexual. Using the word *lifestyle* to describe all homosexual behavior fails to make these distinctions. Neither the term *homophobia* nor *lifestyle* should be used indiscriminately.

> *Objection 2:* "Civil rights" are not at issue when objections are raised concerning the ordination of persons engaged in unrepentant homosexual practice. Christian ministry is not a civil right. Therefore, ordination to Christian ministry is not a civil rights issue.

The Declaration rightly points out that standing against the ordination of homosexuals is not an issue of civil rights. State laws do not dictate whom the church may and may not ordain. Perhaps supporters of the ordination of gays and lesbians could rightly point out that the church's action against them is consistent with or parallel to the violation of rights in the civil arena. Surely, however, neither side wants the state to dictate the church's morality or its decisions regarding who can be ordained. If the state were allowed to make these decisions for us, the integrity of the church would be undermined across the board. I agree with the writers of "A Princeton Declaration" that those who support the ordination of homosexuals should not invoke arguments of civil rights.

It is also important to note that many people who oppose homosexuality (including the ordination of homosexuals) on moral grounds nevertheless support the civil rights of homosexuals (such as the right to adequate health care, the right to own a home, the right to be free from harassment, etc.). There is, of course, some disagreement on what constitutes gay and lesbian civil rights. One might draw the line, for instance, at the right of a lesbian or gay couple to adopt a child; here the debate can become heated again. Nevertheless, it is of no small significance that some opponents of homosexuality support certain rights of homosexuals as citizens. Those who support the ordination of homosexuals need to avoid the caricature (which often accompanies indiscriminate use of the charge of "homophobia") that portrays all opponents of homosexuality as supporting cruel and even violent activity aimed against homosexuals.

"A Princeton Declaration" speaks against cruelty and prejudice, claiming that "compassion is needed" and reminding those who oppose homosexuality that they "are dealing with human lives." The document, therefore, encourages all who speak against the ordination of homosexuals to be compassionate. While those who agree with "A Princeton Declaration" should not naively expect homosexuals to respond enthusiastically to their stance of loving the sinner and hating the sin, all can agree that a significant distinction exists between those who argue against homosexuality with compassion for human beings and those who do so filled with hatred and malice.

The writers of "A Princeton Declaration" employ another phrase that often plays an important role in the debate, that is, "unrepentant homosexual behavior." This term is often employed in the argument over whether homosexual behavior is learned or given at birth. Although "A Princeton Declaration" does not speak directly to this issue, it needs to be addressed here because it is such a significant source of misunderstanding.

Some people argue that there is clear scientific evidence that homosexuality is an orientation given at birth; others argue that the evidence points in the opposite direction. The question of whether homosexuality is a disposition from birth or a free choice made by individuals is a significant issue that all who care about this debate should pursue. Both sides, however, need to recognize that the answer to this question does not settle the moral issue. Here, perhaps more so than at any other point in the debate, both sides talk past each other. Consider the following claims that are often heard in the debate:

First Claim: Homosexuality is a disposition given at birth. The homosexual cannot "repent" of homosexuality any more than someone can repent of being left-handed.

Second Claim: Alcoholics can claim to be born with a disposition toward alcoholism; pedophiles might claim that this is who they have always been;

a murderer could claim to be born with an uncontrollable rage. None of these people, however, can claim that acting on their disposition is moral. *Third Claim:* Homosexuals cannot be compared to alcoholics or pedophiles if they are not hurting anyone. The actions of affection between two consenting adults who love each other are not at all the same as actions that abuse children or destroy human lives.

Both sides in this conversation are making valid points, but each is making a different claim. A person making the first claim has legitimate grounds to argue that homosexuality is a disposition at birth; not all scientists agree with this conclusion, but there is enough scientific and experiential evidence at least to offer a legitimate argument.

A person making the second claim, however, is offering a different and equally legitimate point. The issue is no longer whether homosexuality is a condition at birth, but whether it is morally defensible. The person making this claim rightly holds that one can believe that homosexuality is a genetic disposition and still believe that it is morally wrong. Christians have never believed that we are moral by virtue of our birth; we are moral by virtue of the grace of God. One *can* point to some conditions that are (arguably) present at birth and that are, nevertheless, not morally defensible, such as pedophilia or a tendency toward alcoholism. The examples used may be extreme ones, but they present clear cases in point, nevertheless.

Finally, a person making the third claim also makes a valid point while moving the logic of the argument in a different direction. What sense does it make to compare the actions of a loving, faithful couple of the same sex, who believe that their love for one another is a gift from God, to the behavior of an alcoholic, a pedophile, or a murderer? Surely the consequences of actions carry *some* moral weight.

The question of whether homosexual orientation represents a free choice or a disposition at birth demands our close attention. Its answer can play a significant role in the moral debate. The moral question for Christians, however, cannot be framed simply by asking whether homosexual orientation occurs at birth; rather Christians must ask, "If it occurs at birth, is it an occurrence ordained by God?"[13] Furthermore, when we analyze the debate over this question, we need to determine whether each side is addressing the same issue or talking past each other. While such analysis may not bring about agreement, it can prevent us from misunderstanding each other, and it can perhaps bring more clarity to our own argument.

> *Objection 3:* We believe that those who favor the ordination of persons engaged in homosexual practice cannot do so by appealing to the Bible as their principal authority. In a world where many different voices compete for our attention and obedience, we must hear and obey the Word of God as attested to in Scripture and the confessions of our church.

People who oppose homosexuality accuse those who support the moral integrity of some homosexual behavior of operating by the standards of the world, rather than following the Bible. Society, they argue, has arrived at a point where sex outside of marriage is acceptable, infidelity is tolerated, casual sex and multiple sex partners are commonplace, and homosexuality is considered a viable option for any who choose it. The church, however, should not follow what society says, but what the Word of God indicates. "In a world where many different voices compete for our attention and obedience," says "A Princeton Declaration," "we must hear and obey the Word of God as attested to in Scripture and the confessions of our church."

Ironically, but not surprisingly, those who support the ordination of homosexuals accuse those who oppose it of listening to a different voice than the Word of God and of operating by the standards of the world. While indiscriminate sexual activity and lax morality certainly exist, society, they argue, also generates prejudicial and cruel attitudes toward people who do not fit society's definition of what is normal. The church, they argue, is reflecting society's bigotry—not the Word of God—when it opposes homosexuality.

One of the problems in the debate is, of course, that both sides claim that their "conviction is grounded in the Word of God." Charges are most often made, however, that those who support the ordination of homosexuals are ignoring the Bible. The writers of "A Princeton Declaration" claim that "those who favor the ordination of persons engaged in homosexual practice cannot do so by appealing to the Bible as their principal authority." Their opponents maintain, however that the argument should not center on whether we are reading the Bible, but on how we are interpreting what we read. Three aspects of biblical interpretation are important for the present debate:

Examining Individual Texts

The framers of "A Princeton Declaration" are right to bring forth specific texts that address the issue of homosexuality. All these texts, however, need to be studied to determine precisely what is at stake in their negative pronouncements and how they apply today. While some new interpretations of biblical texts by those who support the ordination of homosexuals are specious and self-serving, others are insightful and challenging.[14] Furthermore, neither side can rest its case on the meaning of individual passages. One must ask about the application of these texts to our situation today. There are any number of passages in scripture that the church does not apply to our situation today. How we determine which passages are appropriate for today is a question both sides of the debate must address.

Individual Biblical Texts Are Interpreted
in Light of the Gospel

The Reformed tradition has always counseled against reading texts in isolation, believing that scripture interprets scripture. Examining what the Word of God says on moral issues such as abortion, nuclear weapons, capital punishment, and surrogate motherhood demonstrates that we cannot claim that isolated texts determine the Christian response to moral issues. The Word of God revealed in the Bible consists of the entire story of God with God's people, from creation, the fall into sin, salvation, sanctification, and the promised future. Biblical interpretation on moral issues requires that individual texts be put in conversation with what the Bible reveals about the gospel.

Biblical Interpretation
and Christian Ethics

Responsible biblical interpretation requires, as argued above, that one put the texts in conversation with the human story today. Among other factors, that conversation demands clarity on what one believes is the right approach to Christian ethics. It is easier to support the rejection of all forms of homosexual behavior if one employs an ethic of absolute law; that is, an ethic that claims certain behavior is morally wrong no matter what the context, consequences, or quality of the relationships involved. Many people who support the morality of some forms of homosexual activity believe that an ethic of absolute law is inconsistent with the Word of God revealed in the Bible and that a contextual ethic is necessary for recognizing the freedom of God to act in ways outside the letter of the law.

There may indeed be no way to resolve the differences that arise over how we interpret the Bible. One should, however, understand that one's approach to ethics and one's theological interpretation of the meaning of the biblical texts for today are essential elements in reading the Bible to discern the Word of God. Charging that one side of the debate is not reading the Bible curtails the opportunity to examine questions regarding the complex issues involved in biblical interpretation and Christian moral reasoning.

> *Objection 4:* The Bible is unambiguous in its affirmation of the male-female covenantal sexual relationship and its condemnation of homosexual practice. There is a biblical mandate for sexuality. The Genesis creation accounts, the Song of Solomon, the nuptial imagery in Hosea and the texts pertaining to the convenantal nature of God bear witness to God's blessing of the male-female convenantal sexual relationship. The Bible also upholds celibacy in the single life.
>
> Homosexual practice presupposes the unwillingness or the inability to commit oneself either to the intimate and permanent bond between part-

ners who are by nature unalterably different or to a life of celibacy. Homosexual union cannot reflect the bond between God and God's people or Christ and his church, which is a union of partners who are by nature unalterably different.

Although I disagree with the conclusions offered by "A Princeton Declaration" on the issue of homosexuality, I believe that Objection 4 makes an extremely significant claim about human sexual relationships that all thoughtful Christians need to consider.[15] For the framers of "A Princeton Declaration" the male-female relationship is essential to what it means to be human as God created us to be. If they are following Karl Barth here (and I believe they are), they are not suggesting that other relationships such as father to son or female friend to female friend are unimportant. Furthermore, in their affirmation that "the Bible also upholds celibacy in the single life," they clearly acknowledge that not everyone is called into married life. Nevertheless, the male-female relationship reflects God's relationship with humanity in a way that no other human relationship does. We—male and female—are counterparts, one to the other, each complementing the other. The male-female relationship cannot be disparaged. Animosity between men and women, simply because they are members of the opposite sex, is ruled out of bounds.

I agree with this affirmation of the male-female relationship as a fundamental relationship for human beings. Those who would disparage it, those who promote hatred of men by women or hatred of women by men challenge a fundamental tenet of the Word of God. Those who would say that *it does not matter* if one relates sexually to someone of the same sex, to someone of the opposite sex, or to both have missed the Word of God.

There are, however, two points on which I believe "A Princeton Declaration" takes a wrong turn. The first has to do with the assumption that men and women are "by nature unalterably different." Unless one wants to base one's argument exclusively on biology (and, therefore, employ a natural law argument), it is difficult to name the essential differences between men and women. Two women can be far more unlike each other than a particular man and woman discover themselves to be.[16] It is not clear why *only* the male-female relationship reflects God's love for us.

My second objection has to do with the freedom of God. Claiming that God calls persons into two types of relationships—heterosexual marriage or celibacy—undermines the freedom of God to call some persons into other types of relationships, that is, homosexual or lesbian ones.[17] This does not mean, however, that the church should claim that God can call persons into *any* relationships, however sordid or destructive. Not all sexual relationships between consenting adults are moral ones. If, however, a lesbian or gay couple who are faithful members of the church experience their love for another in the context of their love for God and enrich the lives of those around them, for what reason does the church continue to maintain an "intolerable contradiction between their creation as sexual beings and their calling to the Christian life?"[18]

Those who support some forms of homosexual union should not undermine the significance of the male-female relationship. Nevertheless, one can uphold the essential value of the male-female relationship and yet maintain that God calls some persons into homosexual relationships. The affirmation of faithful homosexual unions does not challenge the essential value of the male-female relationship any more than the affirmation of celibacy does.

The Real Moral Dilemma

In the summer of 1996, the three-year study will be concluded, and the Presbyterian Church (U.S.A.) will make a decision on the issues surrounding homosexuality once again at its General Assembly. What will happen once the final vote is taken? What will those of us who support the ordination of homosexuals do if we lose the vote? What will those who reject the ordination of homosexuals do if they lose the vote? For one side the loss would be tantamount to being members of a church that refused to ordain women or African Americans. For the other side, the loss would mean that our church has lost its moral grounding in the will of God. Whichever side loses, that side will fear that the Presbyterian Church (U.S.A.) has ceased to be the church and will perhaps contemplate whether leaving the denomination is in order.

Before acting on such an inclination, both sides might remember Calvin's claim that "though the melancholy desolation which surrounds us seems to proclaim that there is nothing left of the Church, let us remember that the death of Christ is fruitful, and that God wonderfully preserves his Church, as it were in hiding places . . . [*quasi in latebris*]."[19] However devastated one side may be by the outcome of this decision, God will not leave God's self without a witness; the church will continue to exist.

Many faithful Christians have found a way to remain in the church even when it makes serious errors in discerning the will of God. Members of the Presbyterian Church (U.S.A.) did once belong to a church where women were denied ordination, and many faithful Christians in other denominations today find a way to remain in their church while staunchly disagreeing with their denomination's stance on the ordination of women. Regarding the issue of race, Presbyterians should recognize that we *already* belong to a church that has not fully overcome its racist practices. This is not to say that just because we have tolerated sin in the church before, we should do so again. It does mean, however, that Calvin's claim—that we are subject to our brothers and sisters in Christ at the same time that no one can bind our conscience—could help keep the church together after the vote is taken. The tension between these two affirmations (being subject to the decisions of the church and maintaining the freedom to disagree) allows us to continue working within the church even when we lose a very important issue.

One thing is certain: Debate over the issues surrounding homosexuality will not go away. No matter what the vote after the three-year study, it will not represent a final decision. Whichever way the decision goes this time, there will be too many dissenters for the issue to be buried once and for all. It will be brought up again. That, of course, makes us all—no matter where we stand—weary. This is, nevertheless, the way of the church. We continue to struggle to discern God's will in the world. For those of us who find in homosexuality no moral dilemma, the real dilemma resides in the question of whether we can live *together* as members of the one Body of Christ even when divided by an issue on which both sides know with such certainty that they are right.

I do hope that all Christians who address the issues surrounding homosexuality in the summer of 1996 and beyond will agree with one of the final paragraphs of "A Princeton Declaration."

> We acknowledge Jesus as Lord and Savior, bear witness to him and not ourselves, and we ultimately seek to do the will of God and not our own will. Many groups throughout history have substituted other agendas for this central agenda of the Church. Our primary identity rests in our relationship of obedience to God through Jesus Christ in the power of the Holy Spirit. "Homosexual" and "heterosexual" are not terms descriptive of the fundamental Christian identity. As Christians we confess and repent of our sins and our identity rests in our relationship with God whom we worship and serve. We are made new, transformed and called to live lives of obedience to the Gospel.

NOTES

1. Even the world of scholarship, which generally encourages rigorous debate, recognizes that some positions are not academically credible. The political views of a neo-Nazi, for instance, are not going to be given a hearing.
2. John Stuart Mill, *On Liberty* (Indianapolis: The Bobbs-Merrill Company, 1956). *On Liberty* was originally published in 1859.
3. Ibid., 21, 64.
4. Ibid., 24.
5. Ibid., 43, 64.
6. Ibid., 64.
7. Ibid., 25.
8. Some people would be quick to point out that this claim is imprecise; the General Assembly voted to strengthen its stance against the ordination of

"self-avowed" and "unrepentant" homosexuals. I have omitted this language, because it constitutes part of the controversy. I acknowledge, however, that the church ordains lesbians and gay men who have chosen a life of celibacy.

9. The text of the document is only one-and-a-half legal pages long; hence, no page numbers follow quotations. The full title of the document is "A Princeton Declaration: Upholding the PC(USA) in the Decision Not to Ordain Individuals Engaged in Homosexual Practice." While not an official document of Princeton Theological Seminary, this statement was written, signed, and distributed by some members of the Princeton Seminary community.

10. *Homophobia* does not indicate a fear of homosexual persons. Rather, the term indicates an extreme repugnance for homosexuals or homosexual activity that seems out of proportion to identifying it as a sin. Such repugnance, while understandable when aimed at a sin such as pedophilia, which destroys innocent human beings, seems excessive when aimed against an action that produces no victims. Identifying homosexuality as a sin is not necessarily a sign of homophobia; feeling extreme revulsion and loathing toward homosexuals is.

11. This occurs in obvious ways, such as when homosexuals are harassed, beaten up, or murdered by those who oppose their sexual orientation. It also occurs when the sins of homosexuals are deemed far more serious than parallel heterosexual sins. For instance, there have been cases in the church where ministers guilty of acts of infidelity involving heterosexual activity were moved to other churches, whereas ministers guilty of infidelity involving homosexual activity had their ordination revoked.

12. Bishop Finis Crutchfield in the United Methodist Church was a staunch opponent of the ordination of homosexuals. Just prior to dying of AIDS he insisted that he had acquired AIDS by ministering to people with AIDS. It was revealed that he had all his married life led a double life, he was himself a homosexual. See Emily Yoffe, "The Gay Bishop," *Texas Monthly* 15, no. 10 (October 1987): 107ff.

13. See Christopher Morse's comment on this aspect of the debate in *Not Every Spirit: A Dogmatics of Christian Disbelief* (Valley Forge, Pa.: Trinity Press International, 1994), 280. Morse's brief, but powerful discussion of "Being Human Sexually" merits attention. See *Not Every Spirit*, 273–83.

14. Christopher Morse claims that in each text that refers to homosexuality, "what is being condemned is clearly the violation of covenant fidelity and not its expression." *Not Every Spirit*, 280.

15. Although the document does not mention Karl Barth, Barth's rich interpretation of the image of God clearly stands behind its claims. The image of God, according to Barth, has to do with the doctrine of the Trinity, God's relationship to humanity, and *humanity's relationship as male and female*. See *Church Dogmatics*, 3.1, 42 (Edinburgh: T&T Clark). For a critique of Barth's exegesis, see Phyllis A. Bird, " 'Male and Female He Created Them': Gen. 1:27b in the Context of the Priestly Account of Creation," *Harvard Theological Review* 74, no. 2 (1981): 129–59.

16. I thank Cindy Rigby for making this point clear in a lecture she delivered on the topic of gender relations at Princeton Theological Seminary.

17. See Paul Lehmann's comments on homosexuality in *The Decalogue and a Human Future: The Meaning of the Commandments for Making and Keeping Human Life Human* (Grand Rapids: Wm. B. Eerdmans Publishing Co., 1995), 173–77.

18. Christopher Morse, 280.

19. John Calvin, *Institutes of the Christian Religion* 4.1.2, ed. John T. McNeil, trans. Ford Lewis Battles (Philadelphia: Westminster Press, 1960).